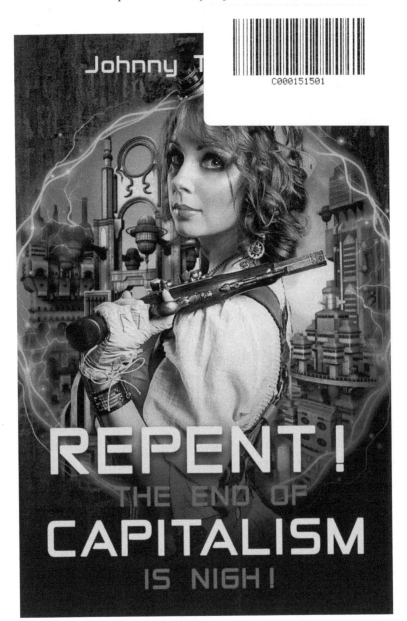

Repent! The End of Capitalism is Nigh!

The lack of affordable housing, a refusal to pay workers a living wage, the push to dismantle and privatize successful government programs like the Postal Service, Social Security, and Medicare. What does it all mean?

These are all "signs of the times," a portent of the End Times...of capitalism.

Capitalism, an economic system dependent on the exploitation of workers and the environment, is doomed to failure. It's only lasted as long as it has because those who benefit most, a mere 1% of the population, wield an ungodly amount of power.

They pit the rest of us against each other, ban books, restrict our bodily autonomy, and buy the loyalty of judges, justices, and politicians. They monopolize mainstream media and frame every discussion of problems to disguise the truth—that capitalism creates inequality as a primary function, not a glitch in the system.

In these essays, author Johnny Townsend (*Recommended Daily Humanity*) helps us adapt to the new reality that awaits as late-stage capitalism collapses around us.

Praise for Johnny Townsend

In *Zombies for Jesus*, "Townsend isn't writing satire, but deeply emotional and revealing portraits of people who are, with a few exceptions, quite lovable."

Kel Munger, *Sacramento News and Review*

In *Sex among the Saints,* "Townsend writes with a deadpan wit and a supple, realistic prose that's full of psychological empathy….he takes his protagonists' moral struggles seriously and invests them with real emotional resonance."

Kirkus Reviews

Inferno in the French Quarter: The UpStairs Lounge Fire is "a gripping account of all the horrors that transpired that night, as well as a respectful remembrance of the victims."

Terry Firma, Patheos

"Johnny Townsend's 'Partying with St. Roch' [in the anthology *Latter-Gay Saints*] tells a beautiful, haunting tale."

Kent Brintnall, Out in Print: Queer Book Reviews

Selling the City of Enoch is "sharply intelligent...pleasingly complex...The stories are full of...doubters, but there's no vindictiveness in these pages; the characters continuously poke holes in Mormonism's more extravagant absurdities, but they take very little pleasure in doing so....Many of Townsend's stories...have a provocative edge to them, but this [book] displays a great deal of insight as well...a playful, biting and surprisingly warm collection."

Kirkus Reviews

Gayrabian Nights is "an allegorical tour de force...a hard-core emotional punch."

Gay. Guy. Reading and Friends

The Washing of Brains has "A lovely writing style, and each story [is] full of unique, engaging characters....immensely entertaining."

Rainbow Awards

In *Dead Mankind Walking*, "Townsend writes in an energetic prose that balances crankiness and humor....A rambunctious volume of short, well-crafted essays..."

Kirkus Reviews

Repent!
The End of Capitalism
is Nigh!

Johnny Townsend

Printed on acid-free paper.

2024

First Edition

Cover design by Breogan Book Covers

Red circular flame by Freepik

Contents

Repent! The End of Capitalism is Nigh!

On July 4th, Radical Women and the Freedom Socialist Party held a labor rally in front of the statue of V.I. Lenin in the Fremont neighborhood of Seattle. Vandals had painted Lenin's hand red to make it look bloody. An unhoused man sat at the base of the statue with a sign clarifying that he was *not* homeless but broke.

Organizers offered to buy him breakfast and watch his belongings while preparing for the rally. They set up the sound system and a literature table with the writings of Clara Fraser: *Socialism for Skeptics*; *Revolution, She Wrote*; and *Socialist Feminism: Where the Battle of the Sexes Resolves Itself.*

A light wind whipped some of the flyers advertising a Feminist Trivia Contest off the table. "People will start throwing rocks soon," someone quipped, "and we can use them as paperweights." But many of these activists had been organizing for years, and someone produced their own bag of rocks to keep papers from flying away.

The rally was small, with perhaps twenty local socialists in the crowd. And that crowd consisted of barely more than thirty people total. A few pedestrians strolling by accepted flyers or bought a copy of the *Freedom Socialist* newspaper, but most averted their eyes and continued walking.

I experienced a bit of PTSD, remembering my time as a Mormon missionary in Rome.

Several folks driving past honked their horns in what I assumed was solidarity, though one driver gave us the finger as he passed with a protracted, angry honk. One of the comrades gave him the finger in return.

A young man with a long beard stood on the edge of the crowd looking intense. There was some kind of symbol on his black T-shirt, but I couldn't quite make it out. Was that the symbol for Extinction Rebellion? Was he a neo-Nazi? An anarchist? Just some random guy from the neighborhood?

With several mass shootings across the country in the preceding days, it was difficult not to feel wary, but the rally continued as planned.

People gave short speeches at the "speak out." One woman talked about bodily autonomy, including abortion and trans rights. Others spoke of labor abuses taking place at PCC and in the City of Seattle. Another speaker reflected on the legacy of Clara Fraser. Someone spoke about the recent Supreme Court rulings banning race-conscious affirmative action and student loan debt forgiveness.

Then came the Open Mic portion of the rally. A union member from Bellevue informed the crowd that state funding for medical clinics had just been reduced from $30 million to $6 million.

Next, the unhoused man who'd sat calmly at the base of the statue for the past hour stood to speak. He suffered from some kind of mental illness and began spouting some incoherent thoughts. At length. A few people in the crowd smiled patronizingly. Others looked uncomfortable.

The man who wasn't homeless but broke then announced his campaign for President of the United States.

Mainstream media often ignores "progressives" but outright bans almost all coverage of socialism. I looked about quickly to see if any journalists had appeared, knowing they'd only show this one clip of the rally to make us all look like "lunatics." Even as a Mormon missionary years earlier, I'd been accused of being one of those crazy men on street corners carrying a sign proclaiming, "Repent! The end of the world is nigh!"

And suddenly, I recognized that the man speaking to us now fully embodied the problems of capitalism. Without universal healthcare, he couldn't receive the mental healthcare services he needed. Without a universal basic income, without housing as a human right, he was condemned to live underneath a statue of Lenin brought over to the U.S. after the fall of the Iron Curtain. Without even a guarantee of food, he was obliged to beg for money from strangers or accept a few dollars from a group of socialists who just happened to be in the neighborhood.

I thought of the spate of scandals over the past few weeks involving billionaire donations to Supreme Court Justices, of their rulings legalizing discrimination against LGBTQ Americans, of their upcoming case that might allow them to outlaw taxing the wealthy.

Climate scientists speak of tipping points past which our climate will be unable to stabilize at conditions humans find survivable.

Capitalism, exploitative by its very nature, has been doomed from the start, but now even those taught from birth to believe it the only viable economic option can see it collapsing before our very eyes.

If we choose to "Repent!" we must remember that part of true repentance includes making amends to those we've wronged.

But whether we repent or not, we'd better prepare, because "The End of Capitalism is Nigh!"

Let's welcome it as we might the Second Coming, because ushering in socialism is our only hope for lasting peace.

Juneteenth rally in Seattle.

Reparations, One Family at a Time

There's been much discussion of reparations over the years and, while several countries have made progress in repairing some of the harm committed against historically oppressed populations, the U.S. government has remained resistant. But as we continue to fight for justice on a larger scale, we can start considering reparations on a personal level. Whether we're white or not, let's ensure our wills leave most of our wealth and property to historically marginalized people.

Most of us have neighbors or coworkers who are black, Latin, Asian, indigenous, or who belong to another marginalized community or ethnicity. They don't need to be our closest relations for us to include them in our will. God knows many of us have biological family members we're not particularly close to, either.

When my partner died in 2005, he didn't leave a will. Since we weren't legally married, his estranged sister inherited the house, the car, the pension, the money in the bank—everything.

When I began another committed relationship a few years later and bought my first home, I immediately consulted an attorney to draw up a will leaving the house to my new partner. But I also included a secondary beneficiary.

If my husband were to precede me in death, the property would go to a friend.

At the very least, we can all ensure that our second beneficiary be someone from a marginalized community.

Studies have revealed that a large part of the wealth gap comes from inherited wealth. A family that's been in a position to pass down even a small amount of wealth, property, or opportunity over generations will have a family member alive today who's been able to attain a strong education and a good job, who probably owns a home rather than rents.

I'd never have earned my first college degree without my family's support, and the down payment on my home was gifted me by my father.

I see a great many people in my position—white, educated, well-traveled, with "good" jobs—who look down on those struggling. "If I can do it, why can't they?" Oblivious to the ways our struggles, real as they are, were lessened by our privilege. I'm still living paycheck to paycheck, after all, and that's with a tremendous head start in life.

Unfortunately, with corporations gaining more control over our lives, even those of us with privilege often have a lower standard of living than our parents. Everyone is struggling these days. And if we have children, we want to ensure they're taken care of first after we're gone. So not everyone will be in a position to pass on wealth to non-family members.

But some of us can. Perhaps we're single. We're childless by choice or circumstance. Perhaps we have children who have done well for themselves and don't need all our money and property. Whatever the situation, some of us *are* in a position to make reparations on a personal level.

We should certainly keep pushing for tuition-free college and vocational training, universal healthcare, subsidized childcare, fare-free public transit, and other policies that help level the playing field and make life more livable for all people.

Most of us already have "causes" we'd like to leave money to, whether that be PBS or Greenpeace or the American Indian College Fund. We want to support organizations that demand the wealthy and corporations pay their fair share of taxes to benefit all of society. There's a lot of competition for every penny we might leave behind.

But let's consider adding the option of transferring some of our wealth to people in our lives from a historically marginalized community.

And let's talk to a neighbor or an attorney today.

Carrying signed petition at City Hall protest in Seattle.

Problem Deniers vs. Problem Solvers

When I was a teenager in the late 1970s, there was already a great deal of talk about overpopulation, though we'd just passed four billion humans on the planet.

My religious leaders would scoff at suggestions that bringing more babies into the world could be damaging in any way. God wanted us to bring as many babies into the world as we could. A popular Mormon musical of the time had certain characters singing about "Zero Population" to demonstrate how corrupt they were.

And this nonsense about running out of room or resources? Why, the lower forty-eight states in the U.S. alone consisted of 1,996,725,760 acres. Divided by four billion, each person could have half an acre to themselves. A family of four would have two full acres. Plenty of room.

Even as a true believer, I wasn't convinced. If we crammed four billion people into the lower forty-eight states as described, they could only be allotted that much space if there were no schools, no restaurants or hospitals or movie theaters. There'd be no room for churches or temples.

There'd be no room for forests, so there'd be few building materials for those four billion people to construct housing. And since there'd be no room for mines to extract ore or factories to refine it, those homes would be meager indeed. There'd certainly be no shipping materials from elsewhere without room for roads or bridges or trains.

If every family of four had two acres to themselves, would those two acres be in the desert? On a mountaintop? In a swamp? In a volcanic crater?

Whether or not the Earth could sustain four billion people, or eight billion, or twelve billion, using such ridiculous statistics suggested that the folks making the argument had no clue what they were talking about. When they then added dismissively, "And in reality there's the rest of the world, too," I had to wonder if they were referring to all those acres in the Sahara and Gobi deserts, in Greenland, in Antarctica...

What struck me as even stranger was that the people embracing this delusion acted as if they were describing heaven. Sounded like hell to me.

Who wanted to live in a world where you were trapped for life on two tiny acres, not even allowed to visit friends or family without trespassing on a neighbor's land? Then again, perhaps trespassing wouldn't be a problem since there'd be no police stations or courthouses or prisons. But what happened when your kids grew up and needed two acres of their own? Would they have to move to Canada or Mexico and start gobbling up acres there?

What happened if you had a fourth or fifth child? Would your neighbors have to move farther away to give you more space, forcing *their* neighbors to move farther away, on and on to the border of the nation?

19

Your kids and grandkids *couldn't* live anywhere close by. All 1,996,725,760 acres were already spoken for.

Often, people who refuse to accept reality will perform extreme mental gymnastics to avoid addressing a crisis. That may get them kudos for their competency in mind games. But deflection doesn't solve problems.

We need problem solvers, not problem deniers.

The first step is acknowledging the problems exist. Too many people on the planet consuming too many resources, and using fossil fuels to do it, meaning even fewer livable areas and resources left for those already here. As hardworking and well-meaning as my Sunday School teachers and other religious leaders were, they weren't up to the challenge.

If we want to solve the problems of overpopulation and climate breakdown, we'll have to think outside the box. That almost certainly means outside the pulpit as well. But whatever the case, that box had better be larger than two acres.

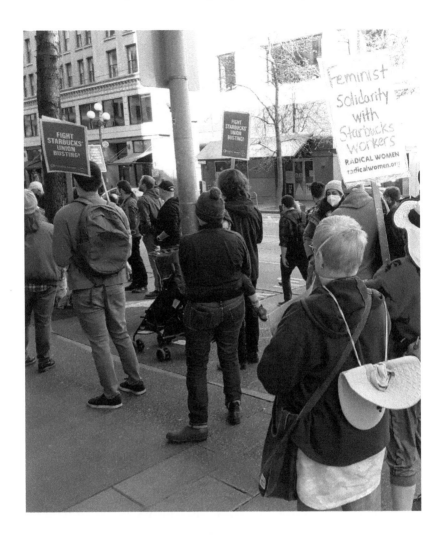

Strike in downtown Seattle.

Oppression Never Gives Up on Its Own

Fifty years ago, on June 24, 1973, a transgender woman from my LDS congregation in New Orleans survived the UpStairs Lounge fire, an arson at a French Quarter gay bar that took the lives of thirty-two people. Regina's partner wasn't so lucky. Neither was Inez Warren, who died along with her two gay sons. Neither was Mitch Mitchell, who initially escaped but ran back in for his partner Horace Broussard. They both died, along with Bill Larson, an MCC minister who burned to death clawing his way through a broken window, and many others.

The fire wasn't a hate crime per se, started by a disgruntled patron who'd been kicked out of the bar earlier that evening. But the New Orleans community joined forces in perpetrating a hate crime after the fact, with religious leaders refusing to bury the dead, with some family members refusing to claim bodies, with witty residents making jokes about "the weenie roast in the French Quarter."

Survivors returned to work the following day, forced to pretend nothing had happened or risk losing their jobs.

Many in the LGBTQ community felt we'd finally "made it" when same-sex marriage was legalized. They believed that society always moves forward, that there's always progress, no matter how slow. They believed that once the old bigots die off, the younger generation will naturally be more inclusive.

What we've seen in recent years is that folks can organize behind fear and hatred quickly. Oppressors understand that the only way to perpetuate their hatred is to recruit the youth. The only way to recruit the youth is to force propaganda on them. And the only way to force propaganda on them is to deny them any access to LGBTQ books in school libraries, to defund public libraries, to censor classroom instruction on LGBTQ history.

They label anyone who simply acknowledges the reality of LGBTQ existence a pedophile, a groomer, a criminal, a monster.

A mere eleven people are behind almost all school library book bans across the nation. Haters organize media reports to inflate their presence so that the rest of us fear being crushed by this overwhelming "majority."

And people *do* back down. Far-right extremists organize boycotts to destroy anyone who steps out of line. They even go after Ted Cruz, surely one of the least woke senators in existence, for saying that executing gay people in Uganda is going too far.

Over the past few decades, the LDS Church has tried to become more mainstream, part of the general Protestant and evangelical community, not understanding that the demon that is hatred will turn on them as quickly as it turned on Target and Chick-fil-A.

When I came out to my fellow congregants many years ago, one announced, "I hate when people tell me they're gay. They always expect me to stand up for them. This is *their* battle."

Another offered more support. "I'll have my girlfriend sleep with you. That'll fix your little red wagon."

I declined the offer.

Another suggested electroshock torture. I declined that offer, too.

My stake president confided, "I don't understand why the Church has a problem with gays, but you've been too public, so I don't have any choice but to excommunicate you."

There's always a choice. They just come with consequences.

A few days ago, a friend in a rural Louisiana parish attended a public library board meeting where the first three speakers insisted the library eliminate all LGBTQ-themed books. Two hundred people in the room sat silently, and my friend felt alone. Scared.

But he stood and spoke up against censorship. Then half the room gave him a standing ovation, thirty people coming up afterward to thank him.

Extremists try to scare our allies into submission. But you're not an ally unless you stand up even when it's uncomfortable. No one needs fair weather allies.

In the series *A Small Light*, we see Miep Gies in Amsterdam rise to the occasion and help hide Otto Frank's family. After the war, she corrected anyone who said she was extraordinary, insisting the claim allowed them an emotional out for doing what she and everyone else is capable of—being an ally even when it's the most frightening thing you've ever done.

Extremists are coalescing efforts against the LGBTQ people in your community and across the nation. We need you to step up and be allies.

Bus Rider in Seattle

Mayor Harrell Must Live Up to Seattle's Values

My escrow shortage this year is over $2000. As a low-level City employee, that's more than a month's take-home pay for me.

Equity and social justice are two of the City of Seattle's core values. Another is accountability. Mayor Bruce Harrell may be a great guy in many ways, but when he and the city council offer workers a 1% COLA (Cost-of-Living-Adjustment) in our upcoming labor contract after 16% inflation over the past couple of years, he's not living up to his values.

City employees are upset, but even more, we're disappointed.

While many on the right rail against "woke ideology," here in supposedly progressive Seattle, we have Mayor Bruce Harrell who demands city workers take what amounts to a 15% pay cut while letting corporations avoid paying their fair share in taxes.

That's not equity. Or social justice. Or accountability.

If I don't have enough money to pay my mortgage, the bank doesn't just shrug and say okay. If I call Seattle City Light and tell them my salary has been cut so I'll have to start paying 15% less on my electric bill, they don't just shrug and say okay.

City employees gathered over 6000 signatures on a petition demanding a fair COLA in the upcoming contract. Bruce Harrell's response?

"You get a 1% COLA."

City employees sent over 1200 emails to the mayor and city council, demanding a response.

Their response?

"You get a 1% COLA."

How City employees are paid has a ripple effect throughout the city, the county, and the state, in both the public and private sector. Everyone's income is impacted when City workers don't get a living wage.

Many departments in the City already operate with a 14% vacancy. They can't find workers to fill jobs to serve residents. Park hours are cut, there are fewer representatives to answer calls, fewer workers to repair lights and roads, to trim trees, fewer workers to pick up trash or repair water leaks. We see how much longer it takes for business owners and homeowners to get permits.

Is this part of Mayor Harrell's plan to "revitalize downtown Seattle"?

City workers aren't asking for a raise when we reject the 1% COLA. We're refusing to accept a pay cut.

Workers want to be able to continue living within city limits so our commute doesn't cut down on family time. We want to continue worshiping and socializing with our neighbors. We want to continue spending at least a few dollars at small businesses in our neighborhoods and support the local economy.

But we can't if Bruce Harrell and the city council insist on cutting our pay by offering a 1% COLA in the face of 16% inflation.

We don't want an 8% COLA. Or 10%. By definition, COLA must match inflation.

If the mayor and city council don't have enough money to pay their workers a living wage, we don't just shrug and say okay. They don't get to stop paying their bills simply because they want to any more than the rest of us do.

And workers' paychecks are one of their bills.

The battle over paying workers a fair COLA is part of a larger issue—prioritizing the self-interest of the privileged over reality.

We're not asking for the world. Just for Mayor Harrell and the city council to live up to their professed values of equity, social justice, and accountability.

Is Lying a Political Issue or a Moral One?

Leaders of The Church of Jesus Christ of Latter-day Saints have repeatedly spoken out against the Equal Rights Amendment, same-sex marriage, medical marijuana, and made declarations on many other hot political controversies, explaining that these weren't political but instead moral issues. They're *obligated* to speak out on moral issues.

One has to wonder, then, if lying is considered a political issue rather than a moral one, because these same leaders never seem to speak up when prominent Mormons lie publicly.

In order to obtain a temple recommend, members of the LDS church must pass a temple worthiness interview. One of the many questions they must answer is, "Are you honest in your dealings with your fellowmen?"

Satan is the Father of all Lies. Liars get sent to the Telestial Kingdom, the lowest order of heaven, and are to be separated from God for eternity. Lying *sounds* consequential.

Ronna McDaniel denies the seriousness of the charges against Trump, claiming the system isn't fair because Hillary Clinton wasn't investigated. She was, of course, at length. Whether you like Trump or not, McDaniel's statements are factually incorrect. And given the gravity of those charges, dangerous.

But do her church leaders take any action toward her?

Even Mitt Romney, the "respectable" Mormon politician, won't criticize his niece when she says the January 6 insurrection was "legitimate political discourse." Is his a lie by omission?

Of course, Mitt Romney has lied publicly as well, editing his opponent's words to say something his opponents never actually said, so what can we expect?

I suppose prominent Mormons could lie during their temple worthiness interviews, but LDS leaders are supposed to have the power of discernment. Even if they don't have that superpower, they certainly have the ability to listen to the public statements these folks make and easily assess they're lying to millions of people.

LDS leaders have long been concerned about PR, excommunicating people who commit sins in such a public way that they "embarrass" the Church. Leaders can't be seen tolerating the bad behavior when the whole world knows about it.

So why do these prominent Mormons who lie repeatedly in public about some of the most serious issues our nation faces keep getting a pass?

Mike Lee has been caught in many public and serious lies. Caught on video planning to cut Social Security and then denying it. Text messages reveal he knew Trump lost the election and still plotted to overturn the results. How *many* serious lies must one tell before it affects one's temple worthiness?

Chris Stewart was literally convicted for lying, and that lie wasn't even his biggest.

Mike Crapo, Jason Chaffetz, Mia Love, and Burgess Owens have all publicly told serious lies of their own. Those lies create misery and suffering for millions. They destroy lives. But neither the lies nor their seriousness seem to be moral issues for the LDS church.

Why is that?

And when the public lies are committed by someone who isn't a politician, as in the case of Glenn Beck, why do those liars get the "it's a political, not moral issue" pass at all?

Even if all these prominent Mormons had been given the Second Anointing and faced no spiritual judgment for any future sins, one has to wonder why the righteous can only succeed in life by behaving wickedly. Or why leaders of God's "one true church" support those who lie like devils.

Is it perhaps because leaders of the LDS church have themselves lied, deceived, and obfuscated about church history and church finances? There's even a common phrase among Mormons: Lying for the Lord. Could the leaders themselves pass a temple recommend interview successfully?

Or avoid excommunication?

If LDS leaders want to regain any degree of trust for their church, they need to start speaking honestly about their own history and finances. If they can't manage that, the least they can do is hold prominent politicians and pundits accountable for lying and embarrassing the church and for deceiving their followers in a reprehensible case of affinity fraud.

If they're unable to do either, perhaps the rest of us should start doubting every damned thing they say.

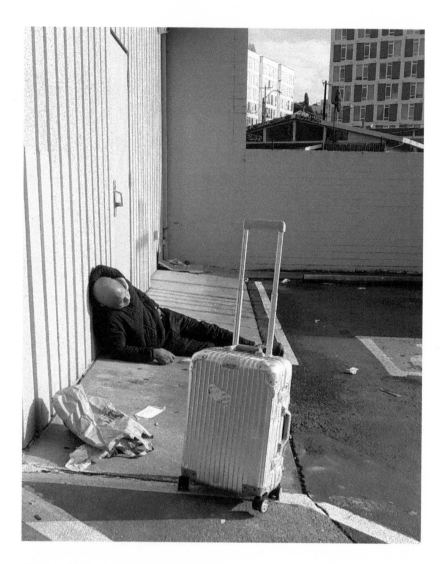

Homeless at the gas station

Misery Loves Company Because Companies Love to Create Misery

"Welfare and food stamps turn people into lazy, weak, immoral bums!" If you're a middle-class political conservative, you've probably said something similar.

But if you're a political conservative, you *already* think people who need these programs are lazy, weak, and immoral.

"Universal healthcare, subsidized childcare, and tuition-free college will turn America into a hellscape!"

But you *already* think America is a hellscape *without* these programs.

"Leftists want to take money from the military to spend on housing, rehab, and mental healthcare!"

But you *already* spend more on the military than any other nation and *still* never feel safe or secure because you're surrounded by the homeless, addicts, and mentally ill.

"Socialism makes people selfish and unmotivated and it takes away personal responsibility!"

But you *already* think the people you don't like are selfish, unmotivated, and irresponsible.

So what exactly are you gaining by denying assistance to those who need it?

"These people want to spend *our* tax money on high-speed internet access and fare-free public transit!"

Just *how* does living in a world where people can't shop for groceries online or get to their workplace without hours of dreariness benefit you?

The "others" in your life remain poor, hungry, sick, unhoused—and miserable.

You need to live among those homeless, poor, unhappy people, and *you* are the ones telling everyone how unhappy you are about it.

So your "conservative" policies make *everyone* unhappy, *by your own admission.*

You do seem sometimes to get a certain degree of satisfaction—not happiness—from ensuring that others suffer, but you're still suffering, too.

And why? Because the wealthiest 1% of our population has tricked you into believing that if you're as cruel as they are, you'll somehow end up as rich as they are. -

But you won't. Because that's not how capitalism and oligarchy work.

We're too willing to accept that cruelty is magically transformed into kindness because doing so allows us to believe we'll be rewarded, either here or in the afterlife, despite the blatant gloating from pundits, politicians, and preachers that proves beyond any doubt there's no kindness involved.

That's how brainwashing works.

Look, I've been brainwashed before, just as you are now. I was a Mormon missionary for two years, which is as close as you can get to being in a cult without using the word. It took years to overcome the mindset I'd been taught over decades.

But once you recognize deceit and manipulation, you can't unsee it.

It's painful to realize the people you love and trust have deceived you, even more painful to accept that you willingly passed on the false information.

But the alternative is to continue to live under oppressive lies and become complicit in forcing that oppression onto others, unhappy without understanding that your unhappiness isn't accidental or a personal failing on your part but intentional on the part of those in power.

Most of you who need to won't read this. Those who do will resist accepting the truth, trying to find fault with my wording rather than facing the undeniable. But you already know that the truth will set you free.

"If I can't have happiness, then no one will!"

Even in a world filled with cruelty, you can be happier if you choose not to be one of the people adding to that cruelty.

It's up to you to set yourself and others free.

Cold and homeless on the bus in Seattle.

Humans Caused This Disaster!

"Humans caused this disaster! Not climate change!"

After the horrific flooding in Libya caused by the collapse of two dams during heavy rains, many climate change deniers (and even some climate change commentators) are claiming it was corruption and poor infrastructure that led to the deaths of more than 11,000 people.

These folks made similar comments regarding the devastation in New Orleans after the levees burst during Hurricane Katrina. "It's not a natural disaster! It's a man-made disaster!"

While it's true that authorities are responsible for not maintaining the two dams that burst near Derna, it's also true that without heavier than usual rains, the lack of maintenance wouldn't have had catastrophic consequences.

Climate change doesn't take place in a vacuum. It's happening all over the world, where there are corrupt governments, governments without resources, incompetent governments. It's happening where there's strong infrastructure *and* where there's weak infrastructure.

"Corruption" takes on multiple meanings when the richest nations in the world, with the best infrastructure, are also the nations subsidizing and extracting the most fossil fuels.

Even in rich countries like the U.S., climate breakdown is devastating. Texas, one of the richest states in the country, saw its electrical grid fail during a winter storm. California has one of the strongest economies in the entire world, but the decision not to cut the power near Paradise led to that city's almost total annihilation. A similar poor decision in Hawaii led to the tragedy in Lahaina.

Much of New Orleans was built on landfill, below sea level. With or without climate change, that probably wasn't wise.

In rich nations across the world with well-funded infrastructure and reasonably democratic government, humans still build too close to the coast. They still destroy wetlands. They still import non-native grasses that increase wildfire risk. They still build in valleys that act as wind tunnels during firestorms. They still do many things that exacerbate every natural disaster.

Humans are the main cause of climate change, so no matter what specific act of corruption or failed infrastructure or poor planning or mismanagement contributes to any given disaster, humans make up two of the three ingredients for every disaster. The "natural" part exists because climate and weather exist. But humans pumping out greenhouse gases transform the "natural" disaster into unnatural proportions.

It's impossible to separate natural disasters from man-made disasters because we are bound together through our interactions with nature and one another.

We exploit resources to gain personal wealth. We destabilize other nations to take advantage of their resources. We go to war over oil. We create the instability which ensures that any natural disaster, even before amplification by climate change, will be catastrophic.

Even in a near-perfect world, where our only sin was the continued use of fossil fuels, we'd still be responsible for the deaths, injuries, and property loss from the heavier rains, stronger storms, and hotter heatwaves ravaging communities across the planet.

We can't dismiss the impact of climate change simply because it affects imperfect humans. There's no city, state, or nation made of perfect clones of Jesus Christ (or whoever the perfect person in your religion or mythology might be).

Mistakes are part of the human condition. Will we *only* consider death and calamity the result of "real" climate disaster if it happens in a utopia?

When fossil fuel corporations and their allies frame death and misery as man-made, let's amplify that framing by pointing out that the "men" responsible for that death and misery are the CEOs and shareholders of every fossil fuel company wreaking havoc on the environment.

Gay Romance Novels and the Reality of Unaffordable Housing

I may not be the "hopeful romantic" Joan Wilder is, but after watching the Hindi series *The Railway Men*, about rail workers risking both their careers and their lives to save victims of the Union Carbide gas leak in Bhopal, or reading books on the climate crisis such as *We're Doomed. Now What?* I sometimes crave a bit of light reading. Relaxing with over three dozen gay romance novels this year, I've discovered that even in the world of beach literature, stark realities seep through. Again and again, no matter where in the world these stories are set, the cost of housing is so problematic that the only way protagonists can afford to survive is by inheriting wealth or receiving an insurance payout.

Sure, a few of the protagonists, despite growing up poor, are determined "to succeed" and somehow, through sheer grit, manage to become financially successful. Suspending disbelief, we accept the magic of grit as if it's a viable solution to exploitation and income inequality. We take the author's word that this is a realistic story, not fantasy fiction.

But even in these novels celebrating the miracle of soulmates, enduring love, and happily ever afters, most authors are forced to introduce literature's latest *deus ex machina*—stable housing.

The authors I've read this year were both male and female, white and black, gay and straight (and possibly other variations). They were of different ages and nationalities. But despite the diversity, another consistent theme was the failure of capitalism as an economic system. Stories set in the 1950s and 1960s talked of McCarthyism, Marxism, and Communism. Protagonists came from socialist homes. Stories set in the present mentioned labor struggles.

Most authors went out of their way to show sensitivity to gender issues, sexual orientation, race, autism, PTSD, depression, and various other "differences" for which people suffer discrimination. Many characters even made statements such as, "Last night I looked online and discovered…" so that the authors could clumsily reveal their research.

But the anti-capitalist themes felt more organic. There seemed no attempt to be delicate or politically correct. The attitudes felt natural and unavoidable, like discussing record heat or rising fascism in U.S. politics. Not interpretations. "Just the facts."

Here's a snippet from a workplace conversation in the charming *10 Things That Never Happened* by Alexis Hall, set in the UK:

> Tiff looks at me with more disappointment than you should be allowed to direct at somebody who's nearly ten years older than you and also your boss. "This is exactly what is wrong with late-stage capitalism."

"Y'know," I say, "you're very Marxist for a trainee hairdresser."

"Hair and beauty consultant," she corrects me, "and isn't the whole point of Marxism that it's a philosophy for ordinary working people?"

Later, as the main character, Sam, argues with his boss, Jonathan, over profit and the exploitation of workers, we get this exchange:

"It sounds like you're saying you want me to treat the staff like crap."

"I want you to prioritise targets."

"I do prioritise targets," I tell him. "I just don't prioritise them over people."

The expression on his face makes me want to shove a lot more than a pencil up a lot more than his nose. It's the expression you get when your new puppy shits on the floor and you can't be angry at it because you know it can't help itself. "People don't pay your salary. I do."

It's really tempting to point out he's just said he isn't a person. But I'm supposed to be saving my job, not scuppering it. "Well, I don't want to teach my granny to suck eggs, but the people run the shop. The shop makes the money, and the money is how you pay me. So in a way they do."

The novel is a comic romance, yet this battle over exploitation and capitalism is the main conflict throughout the story. And frankly, it rings true to the conversations I regularly hear in my own workplace.

From Marshall Thornton's *Sentenced to Christmas*, another comic romance, we get a main character whose father has been on the run from authorities for decades because of his "radical" activity in the 1960s and 70s. The premise gives us a defendant who's ordered to spend the holidays with a prosecuting attorney so he can learn the true meaning of Christmas:

> "Judge Winthrop probably wants to hear something along the lines of Christianity being the best religion in the world, Jesus is White, Santa is too, the war on Christmas is real, throw in a dash of American exceptionalism, veiled racism, greed is good and God Bless America the most Christian country in the world."

The story is a cross between *The Importance of Being Earnest* and *La Cage aux Folles*, a farce, and yet it's set firmly in the real world of capitalism as religious dogma because nothing could be more ridiculous than seeing abuse as divine.

M.A. Wardell's *Mistletoe & Mishigas* is set in Portland, Maine, where housing isn't typically as expensive as in many other parts of the country. Yet the main character, Sheldon, and his sister, Naomi, must share an apartment. "We can barely make our rent some months between our two paltry salaries." He's a schoolteacher and she's a nurse, but their combined income is still not enough to make ends meet.

Even minor characters in these novels bring out the recurring issues. In Bryan T. Clark's *Hawthorne Manor*, the protagonist asks his boyfriend about another couple he's just met.

> In the parking lot, Tucker and Dancer got into a black Porsche 911. He watched as Dancer dropped into the driver's seat of the sports car.
>
> "What does Dancer do for a living?" Elliot eyed the beautiful car.
>
> "He works a lot with the homeless. His mother died. She was a famous author and left him everything. You know those yellow-and-green mobile shower trailers you see all around the city that the homeless use to shower and wash their clothes in? That's all him. Dancer financed the whole project."

At the end, one of the protagonists inherits $1,000,000 from the man he's been working for. The other protagonist inherits $28,000,000. They then purchase the man's home, located in the Pacific Heights neighborhood of San Francisco. Their former employer has also left money to support homeless shelters across the city and to construct and run an LGBTQ senior living facility.

We get miracles because increasing numbers of authors and readers understand that under late-stage capitalism, there's no realistic way to solve these problems.

In Cat Sebastian's *We Could Be So Good*, one of the main characters, Andy, inherits his job as owner and editor of a major New York newspaper in the late 1950s. Despite the privilege, Andy and his father are "progressive" and come from a family of Marxists. And despite the time period, when "affordable" housing was more accessible than it is today, the author still has Andy inherit property. The protagonist also receives a large payout from his mother's life insurance. When he and Nick face an uncertain future after being targeted by the police because of their homosexuality, Andy resolves the problem by purchasing the four-story apartment building Nick lives in. You know, the way everyday gay couples avoid the risk of eviction.

That said, it's one of the best gay romance novels of the year. Even the best authors are forced on some level to deal with the reality of unaffordable housing. After all, while the book is set in 1958, fans are reading it today.

In *The Secret Lives of Country Gentlemen*, set in England during the Napoleonic wars, author K.J. Charles has one protagonist, a poor clerk in London, inherit a country manor from his estranged father. Sir Gareth falls for a biracial smuggler, Josiah, who helps him see the world through a different lens.

> He'd met plenty of radicals in London—men who wanted wealth redistributed, laws changed, the government made representative. Joss Doomsday, fervent patriot of a hundred square miles of marshland, was perhaps the most radical man he'd ever met.

Anachronistic or not, the same themes permeate this story as well.

With Bernie Sanders running for president twice, with the failure of corporations to address the climate crisis, with COVID forcing us to see universal healthcare as a basic human right, with the increasing number of labor strikes, with the unhoused population exploding in the U.S., with all the other political and economic crises compounding every struggle, there's been a sea change in public consciousness regarding capitalism.

Even in *Muscle Cub: A Bear Camp Novel* by Slade James, set during a sex party weekend in rural Georgia, the formerly taboo word "socialism" pops up in casual conversation.

> "You like to think there's a sense of community the minute you set foot on the property, but after a whole weekend of partying together, it was a moment of, like...spontaneous democracy. Socialism, maybe?"

Several of the stories, including *In the Gray* by Christina Lee and *Deep Dish* by Lori Witt, went so far as to feature unhoused protagonists. Those who didn't inherit wealth or rise to financial success through "hard work" simply ended up on the streets. And yet still found romance because these were, after all, romance novels.

Most of today's older generation was raised to believe socialism was evil and Satanic, but younger Americans have a far more positive view. And the failures of capitalism have become so apparent that folks of all ages are rethinking our attitudes toward labor and economic equality.

If we don't feel up to taking a class on the subject or attending a rally, we can still get an introduction into our new shared consciousness by picking up some light reading. *The Art of Husbandry* by Jay Hogan is a great place to start, where we can fantasize about inheriting several hundred acres of land in the Southern Alps of New Zealand and leaving the madness of urban housing prices behind.

As long as we don't lose the farm.

Let's Make a Paradigm Shift Toward Socialism

Let's say we have a friend who doesn't need money. His spouse has a good job or she's saved enough for herself already or he inherited money or whatever. She doesn't need to work.

But our friend chooses to take a part-time job so she can feel productive, so he doesn't feel disconnected from the world.

Question: Are we proud of our friend for their decision? Impressed with their work ethic? Are they doing a "good" thing?

My former fiancée in southern Italy posed this question shortly after accepting my proposal (it followed the more important question I had to answer first—did I like my pasta *al dente* or "overcooked"). As an American raised with a Protestant work ethic, a Mormon who believed in working hard to enter heaven, a Republican raised in a right-wing family, I told Nicla that yes, I was impressed with her friend's decision.

Then Nicla posed another question: Since southern Italy had an unemployment rate of 18%, shouldn't her friend find fulfillment doing volunteer work instead of taking a job someone else needed?

My understanding of what was good and moral and praiseworthy changed instantly.

We've all experienced similar moments when we've realized the way we've long looked at a particular issue wasn't perhaps the best way. We've learned. We've adjusted. If the epiphany was large enough, we experienced a paradigm shift.

Sometimes these shifts are painful, but more often, they're liberating. A woman I know suffered for decades with feelings of failure because of her schizophrenia. If she was stronger, she believed, this wouldn't have happened to her. Adopted as an infant, she'd never known any biological family, but when she neared sixty, she finally took a DNA test.

My friend discovered numerous blood relatives, many of whom also dealt with either schizophrenia or bipolar disorder. The realization that her mental illness wasn't her fault but had a clear genetic link lifted an enormous weight from her, allowing her to accept her diagnosis and the medications to treat it.

We can be similarly energized by paradigm shifts, better able to tackle problems and work toward goals with more energy. Because that new knowledge we have is powerful.

Many of us have experienced paradigm shifts when it comes to race or religion or sexual orientation. Our understanding of the basic principles changes. There may have been a slow accumulation of information leading to it, but there was also an a-ha moment when our views shifted suddenly and drastically.

Every day, more of us are experiencing similar shifts in our understanding of the limitations of capitalism. The system was unquestionably better than what came before, but that doesn't mean it's the epitome of human ingenuity. Societal need has moved beyond the best that capitalism can offer.

We've seen the difficulty in earning an education, the near impossibility in purchasing a home, the friends and neighbors crushed by medical debt. We've witnessed how the criminal justice system doesn't function to protect everyday citizens but to protect the property and privilege of the wealthy. We've seen that capitalists never have enough money to support life but always have plenty to fund war.

Beyond all that, we've seen that capitalism is incapable of dealing with the existential threat of climate breakdown. An economic system dependent on profit—particularly short-term profit—and the exploitation of humans and resources will *always* choose profit and exploitation over stabilizing the climate. That's not a glitch in the system. It's the fundamental way this system operates.

Most of us have slowly been growing more aware of this reality, the way we hear a low rumbling we suspect might be a truck in the distance, a rumbling that grows steadily into a roar until we recognize a plane is about to crash into our home.

The sooner our brain accepts the shift in paradigm, the sooner we can take action. Whatever our most pressing personal need is—education, housing, healthcare, criminal justice, peace, climate—we won't be able to make meaningful progress until we move past capitalism. It's not that socialism is merely a *better* way. Success simply can't happen at all under capitalism. Even those previously (partially) successful democratic socialist countries in Europe are faltering now under capitalism. The social contract to care for one's citizens simply cannot compete with the drive for ever more profit.

It's likely that someday, humans will move beyond socialism as we've moved beyond feudalism and capitalism. But socialism is the next step forward, and once we understand and accept this paradigm shift, we can't unsee it any more than a geologist can unsee their understanding of plate tectonics, any more than a paleontologist can unsee the relationship between birds and dinosaurs, any more than the Pope can unsee the structure of the solar system.

Paradigm shifts have happened repeatedly throughout history, followed by huge advances in whatever field they've occurred. The facts were often known and resisted for decades before finally becoming universally accepted. We must incorporate the reality that's been plain to see for well over a century already.

The time for capitalism has come and gone. It's time now to embrace socialism.

Living in RVs in Seattle

A Moment of Noise Is Better Than a Moment of Silence

Recently, I emailed a gay friend in Canada about a report that had just come out evaluating the police response to the school shooting in Uvalde, Texas that left nineteen children and two teachers dead. It was clear even at the time of the shooting that the response was poor, but the report analyzed just how astonishingly poor it was.

377 officers from various forces were on the scene, many for 77 minutes before confronting the gunman. We'll never know how many of the injured could have been saved if they hadn't been allowed to bleed out. Some officers were heard on bodycam admitting they were afraid to go into the classroom because the shooter had an assault weapon. Well before finally doing their job, one officer shouted into a classroom where many children had already been killed, asking, "Is anyone in there?"

A young girl called out, "Yes!" certainly hoping she was about to be rescued.

But she wasn't. The officers continued to work up their courage to go in. Meanwhile, the shooter, who'd also heard the girl, was now able to locate and kill her.

My friend's response to the report?

55

"When you want to 'Defund the Police,' this is what you get."

I was flabbergasted. I knew he was friends with some MAGA Canadians (yes, there are way too many Trump supporters up there), and I've tried to gently correct him when he's made misogynistic comments in the past. Even gay men who've faced years of discrimination are often biased against people who aren't like them.

My friend's comment warranted another gentle correction. His words couldn't stand unchallenged, yet letting him know just how thoroughly awful I thought his view was wouldn't likely help, either.

I emailed back: "It's fascinating the way different people can see the same information and interpret it so differently. When I see 377 officers refusing to save the kids because they were afraid of the gunman, I don't see an underfunded police force. I see a police force that spends lots and lots of money on officers who are fine with harassing people of color but who don't do the job the public believes they're supposed to do—protect them. This was Texas, after all. There was zero defunding of any police department in that state. And those officers weren't afraid of being accused of police brutality if they shot the gunman. *They* were afraid of being shot by an AR-15. But we don't need to agree on that point."

I then concluded by making some positive comments about another topic he'd mentioned in his previous email.

Did my correction make a difference? I rather doubt it. But it's still important, I think, not to let these types of statements go unchallenged. I've done far too much of that in my life already and now understand that remaining silent isn't a neutral act. It's not diplomacy or discretion. It's not tact. It's complicity.

Has a friend or family member said something dismissive about the way a rape victim was dressed? Have they said something disparaging about Latinos? About workers struggling to pay their student loans? It's almost impossible for everyone in our circle (or ourselves) to have reached a level of "enlightenment" about every oppressed or marginalized group. And it can feel like an overwhelming task to correct misconceptions and question biases every time we hear an inappropriate comment.

But what's the alternative?

And how useful is silence?

I don't know about you, but I don't feel particularly powerful. Marches and rallies and protests "bring attention" to a problem. They "put pressure" on government officials, but they are rarely enough to counteract the pressure from oligarchs.

When I receive fundraising emails from progressive or even socialist politicians pointing out that their opponent has corporate donations in the tens of millions, I can't help but think donating $20 to the better candidate will have little useful impact.

Will my vote even count if there's no paper trail? If losers outright lie about the results?

But I do donate $20. I do participate in rallies and protests. I do vote.

While we may not have much power to impact state or federal policy, we can push back when friends, family, and coworkers make biased or otherwise damaging comments.

We don't need to be obnoxious. But we can be firm. And even if we're not good at speaking under pressure, we can set boundaries and enforce them. "You will not say that kind of thing around me." That alone sends an important message.

At a recent tribute to a local labor activist, another labor leader said, "Let's not offer a moment of silence in Kirk's honor but a moment of noise." We spent the next minute chanting labor slogans.

Unless the aliens from *A Quiet Place* have invaded our neighborhood, silence is rarely useful. Let's instead use our voices, and amplify the voices of the marginalized, to challenge injustice and bias whenever we encounter it.

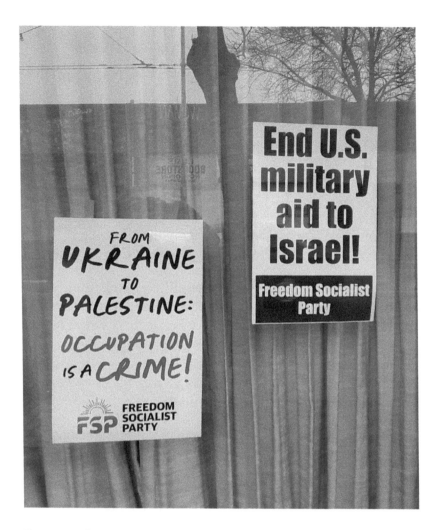

Protest signs

Support Seattle Workers Who Serve Seattle Residents

We make nuanced decisions throughout our lives. Choices aren't always easy.

But in the current contract negotiations between City of Seattle officials and City workers, the right decision is clear.

Mayor Bruce Harrell, Director of Labor Relations Shaun Van Eyk, and the city council have decided to "offer" workers the worst contract local labor leaders have seen in decades. At a recent three-hour bargaining session, City officials eliminated all "small table" issues from discussion. They reiterated their offer of a 1% COLA (Cost-of-Living-Adjustment) in the face of 16% inflation.

Union leaders walked out of the bargaining session after only twenty minutes.

For the most part, I enjoy working for the City. I have a public-facing job and strive to give people a positive experience when they visit our site. I love offering tips and additional information that leave people with a smile. It's genuinely rewarding.

Most of us are here because we love what we do.

That doesn't mean we're happy about working for inadequate compensation.

When I first began working for the City six years ago, I learned about the Race and Social Justice Initiative. Every vendor contract had to be vetted through a Race and Social Justice lens. Each decision we made about programs, worksites, community centers, bike lanes, or anything else impacting the community had to be made after consulting with the community. Seattle has some of the most diverse demographics in the country. We couldn't simply impose what we thought best on others without first seeking input.

Beyond that, every employee was required to attend classes and workshops on unconscious bias. We watched short videos on a weekly basis, read articles, held monthly discussions in small groups.

We faltered a lot. People felt uncomfortable. The program wasn't a blazing success. But we were trying to create an equitable workplace and a city that valued social justice.

We understood that it might not be possible to succeed in this endeavor completely. But it meant something to the workers that we were at least trying.

Now, though, Mayor Harrell, the city council, and other officials are deliberately codifying injustice into the new labor contract with City employees.

We've moved from confronting unconscious bias to consciously hurting workers and, by extension, the residents those workers serve.

Seattle is an expensive city. Our minimum wage is higher than that of many cities and states in the nation. So at first glance, it might sound like workers earn plenty of money. What are we complaining about?

Well, we can't pay our bills. We can't afford one-bedroom apartments, much less larger ones if we dare to start families. A recent article in the *Seattle Times* revealed that in order for a resident to purchase even a "starter home" in the city, he or she would need to earn $142K a year.

I don't expect the Labor Contract Fairy to get me a 450% raise to reach that mythic level of income, but when City officials offer workers a 15% pay cut despite fully understanding our struggles, their behavior is as morally bankrupt as that of any fairy tale villain.

We face historic vacancy rates up to 14% in many departments. The City can't keep workers who can no longer afford to live close to their jobs. The City can't attract new workers to take their place. When your rent is 50% of your take-home pay every month, you can't afford to eat out. You can't afford to support small businesses in your neighborhood.

You can't afford to do anything other than survive. You certainly can't thrive.

And what does that 14% vacancy rate mean for other Seattle residents?

There are fewer workers at Seattle City Light or Seattle Public Utilities to answer phones or respond to customer requests or complaints. Fewer workers to trim weeds, blackberries, or bushes in public areas. No one comes to repair broken lights on the outdoor tennis courts.

Internally, City workers often wait two, three, even four months for repairs as well. Some of our credit card readers go down for weeks at a time. Our computers routinely go down.

Currently, there are vacancies for librarians and for security officers who work at libraries. There are vacancies even for top positions like Director of Administrative Services, Director of Library Programs and Services, and Director of Human Resources and Labor Relations for the library. When you can't even keep people at the top, there might be a problem.

SPU can't find water treatment operators or field techs. One of their job listings for Pump Station Electrician says "first consideration given to candidates who apply by February 28, 2023." Over five months later the position still hasn't been filled.

There are job vacancies at the Animal Shelter, which takes care of 5000+ animals a year. Those vacancies delay spaying and neutering. They impact adoptions and pet licensing.

In the Parks Department, the City needs boat ramp operators, lifeguards for the pools, folks to lead summer camps.

Local businesses can't get the permits they need as quickly as when we're fully staffed. Neither can homeowners. The effects of the high vacancy rate are wide ranging, given the large scope of services the City provides.

The City needs to hire more 911 dispatchers. It needs more marshals at the Seattle Municipal Court. Much is made of the shortage of police officers, as if that department is facing a vacancy rate the other departments aren't facing.

The City can't keep enough workers in *any* department.

Low morale among City workers often leads to more absenteeism, which impacts both the employees and the public. It also leads to more workers looking for other jobs, further impacting the vacancy rate. Workers who want to stay are burdened with doing extra work to keep their department running, and when that extra workload lasts month after month after month, it takes a toll of its own.

Coming on the heels of the pandemic, when public-facing employees were under constant stress from other workers retiring early, quitting, calling in sick, and even dying, that only adds to the cumulative stress.

If our city is becoming a dystopia, it's not because people are choosing to live in tents and RVs to follow the latest trend. It's because money is going to corporations, not people. That's a choice our leaders have made.

City workers pay sales tax like everybody else. We pay property tax. If Mayor Harrell and the city council can only provide even our inadequate infrastructure by funding it with a 15% cut in the paycheck of every worker, that's not okay.

It's not effective, either.

Poor people can't pay for a functioning infrastructure. Neither can the middle class. The money must come from those who have it—the wealthy and the corporations they run. That's not an ideological stance. It's simple math.

These are all problems exacerbated by City leaders like Mayor Harrell, the city council, and the Director of Labor Relations. City workers aren't to blame. We *want* to serve the public. That's why we're here.

Our contract expired at the end of 2021, more than eighteen months ago. We've had an *additional* 3.2% inflation just since January.

The City has refused to negotiate in good faith for the new contract. We've signed petitions, emailed letters to the mayor and city council, and written op-eds, but the City refuses to give us a fair COLA or address our other concerns.

We need help putting pressure on City officials.

Across the country, workers are standing up for themselves in ways they haven't in years. UPS drivers, Starbucks employees, Amazon warehouse workers, hotel workers, sanitation workers, actors, screenwriters, folks in a wide variety of fields, have united to make quite reasonable demands.

We're okay with other people being rich. We just need enough to pay our monthly bills without joining the hundreds of thousands of other homeless folks filling our cities across the nation.

The solution for the systemic injustices in our country are beyond the scope of any individual contract, but each of these labor contracts is an important piece of that solution.

Alaska Airlines flight attendants rallying at Seatac airport need support getting a fair contract.

King County Metro workers in labor negotiations need a contract that doesn't eliminate their right to file a grievance when they've faced discrimination in the workplace.

We need to get *better* at protecting rights, not worse.

The next public event to demand a fair contract for City of Seattle workers is a rally at City Hall on September 19. If you can be there, please come. If you can take care of your neighbor's kids so your neighbor can come, please babysit.

If you can call the mayor's office, please call. If you can write a letter to the editor, please write.

Solidarity comes in many forms. Ultimately, we're all in this together against the politically powerful and the wealthy who fund their campaigns. A city can't function without infrastructure and the workers who maintain it.

We're here because we want to work, and because we want to serve. Please help us to help you.

Personal Responsibility for Conflating Love with Cruelty

Some of my closest family members treat me badly because their church tells them to. I long tried to excuse them because I remembered when I was deceived by the LDS church as well.

Then I remembered I Corinthians 10:13, "There hath no temptation taken you but such as is common to man: but God is faithful, who will not suffer you to be tempted above that ye are able," and I realized that at some point, we're all responsible for our own abusive behavior, no matter what cultural mindset we've been immersed in.

When I assigned my students Shirley Jackson's "The Lottery," many were shocked and outraged to imagine a society that could act as cruelly as the one depicted in the story. Then I asked if they could imagine a future historian looking back on *our* time and saying the same thing. "What do *we* do routinely in our culture someone else *might* consider unacceptable in the future?"

After some heated discussion, students suggested head injuries in football, boxing matches, and horse racing. Others then suggested boiling lobsters alive or big game trophy hunting. Next came a lack of universal healthcare, long prison sentences for non-violent drug offenses, and forcing students to take on decades of student loan debt.

Subsidizing fossil fuel corporations and the destruction of our climate.

The students began *thinking*, which is all a teacher can really hope for.

But if my students could begin reassessing acceptable morality after one short story and a single class discussion, we're all in a position to do at least a minimal amount of self-reflection.

As a Mormon missionary in Rome, I was assigned to guide "greenies," new missionaries who'd just arrived from the U.S. When one of them wasn't performing at a level my zone leaders deemed acceptable, I was ordered to hound the man until he got in line.

In this closed, cult-like culture, peer pressure and conformity were powerful forces, but I simply couldn't follow the directives of my leaders. I instinctively knew it was wrong to treat my missionary companion badly. If he was sinning, that was his prerogative. After all, in the Pre-Existence when Lucifer offered to force everyone to be good, Heavenly Father rejected that plan.

So when modern LDS leaders—apostles and prophets—urge members of their church to disinherit their children who don't attend services faithfully, when they urge members not to accept their children's same-sex partners, when they urge members to behave in other cruel ways, those church leaders are responsible for leading their followers to sin. But those followers are responsible for agreeing to *commit* those sins.

"There is beauty all around when there's 'tough love' at home."

Doesn't quite have the same ring as the popular hymn. And justifiably so.

Mormons discount Brigham Young's acceptance of slavery because "he was a man of his times." But even in the time of Brigham Young, there were abolitionists who could look past societal norms. He was responsible for choosing not to do so.

Cruelty is cruel, no matter who tells us otherwise. Shrugging off our personal responsibility when we hurt family members—or complete strangers—cannot be the guiding principle in the lives of people who hope to become gods.

Of course, it's easy for me to see the flaws of my family members who treat me badly. That's hardly a stretch. Their behavior is blatantly obvious.

What's harder is to examine the ways I'm also conflating love with cruelty, or complacency with cruelty, or ignorance with cruelty.

We can't turn into paragons of 100% virtue overnight, but we can tackle one blind spot at a time and become a tiny bit better as human beings rather than excusing every cruelty just because others do. We can choose to be conscious of and responsible for our personal behavior.

Our devout family members may be tempted by LDS leaders and LDS culture to behave cruelly, they may be directly led to cruelty, but they'll never tempted or led beyond what they can resist. That's according to their own doctrine, so we can hold them to it.

And we can stop giving them a pass just because they give themselves one.

Socialism as Harm Reduction

As a former Mormon who made a sacred vow in the temple to live the United Order, I still find it difficult to advocate for socialism. In fact, it's *because* I was a member of the One, True Church that I can never be 100% committed to *any* ideology again. The One, Perfect Answer to All Our Problems doesn't exist.

That doesn't mean, however, that some answers aren't *better* than others. There are different protocols for treating cancer, different techniques for raising crops, different approaches to losing weight, different methods for addressing substance abuse.

One of those approaches is Harm Reduction. We may not always be able to *solve* a problem, but we can lessen its harmful impact both on individuals and society.

We'll see the weaknesses of socialism more clearly when we compare them to the even greater weaknesses of capitalism. We won't find the Holy Grail in any economic system, but that doesn't mean we shrug off every abuse we're enduring now.

We don't say, "Nobody's perfect" when our spouse is beating us every night. We leave the abuser or risk being killed.

We can think in terms of a weight loss regimen for an obese person who desperately needs to lose eighty pounds. Socialism might only help that person lose fifty pounds. But capitalism would mean gaining an additional twenty. Sure, socialism may not be the perfect solution for this person, but it serves them far better than capitalism.

In the U.S., we've been taught at school, in our religious institutions, and by pop culture that our income reflects our worth. We get what we deserve. If we don't deserve, we don't get. It's not *our* fault if some people aren't up to the task of proving themselves and end up living in cardboard boxes. That's the choice they made by not stepping up.

Capitalism demands a perpetual state of housing and job insecurity to function. These aren't bugs in the system; they're essential features.

When socialists talk to friends and family, a common response is, "Communism sounds good in theory, but we all know how it worked in Russia." They might then add, "Besides, socialism goes against human nature."

Only we don't know either of these things. What we have is a lifetime of propaganda distorting the facts and framing the results in manipulative ways.

Did Stalin kill people? Yes! Millions of them. Did Mao kill people? Yes. Millions.

So how can anyone possibly support these monsters?

First, communism and socialism aren't the same thing. The fact that most of us don't already know this is a direct result of capitalist propaganda.

More importantly, it's possible to believe in principles even if they're executed by imperfect people. Would any patriotic American say the U.S. did the right thing when killing Native Americans, when enslaving Africans, when conducting unjustified wars in Iraq, Afghanistan, and other countries?

Why wouldn't the same apply to socialists who see the good in socialist economic policy despite the bad moral decisions made by certain socialist or communist leaders?

Critics of socialism rush to point out how many people died under that system. *The Black Book of Communism* details millions of deaths attributable to communism. And the numbers are frighteningly high.

But some of them don't stand up to examination. For instance, the authors include the millions of Soviet and German deaths resulting from the Nazi invasion of Russia. But are socialists truly the ones responsible for those deaths?

It would be like accusing abolitionists in the U.S. for the 650,000 deaths that resulted from the American Civil War. Are people who sought to free enslaved humans really the culprits here or are the slaveowners who treated other humans as property?

Since those 650,000 deaths are directly attributable to capitalism, they must be placed in the corresponding column.

And the tally hardly stops there. *The Black Book of Capitalism* and videos like *The Death Toll of Capitalism* suggest that far more people have been killed as a result of capitalist policies than socialist.

Belgians killed over 10,000,000 people in the Congo.

The British killed over 50,000,000 people in India. Some estimates are double that.

But if hundreds of millions of people can be killed under either economic system, why change what we already have?

It goes back to Harm Reduction.

We aren't just comparing the U.S. to the Soviet Union. Capitalism also includes Kenya and Paraguay and Morocco and India. It includes Italy, where the unemployment rate in the south has hovered between 18% and 25% for the past four decades, with its accompanying poverty, crime, and death.

Just as there's a difference between socialism and communism, it's worth clarifying that socialism and capitalism are both economic systems, not political systems. One can have democracy under either system just as one can have a dictatorship under either system.

In fact, the U.S. has toppled democratically elected leaders in almost forty other countries and installed authoritarian leaders in their place (think Pinochet in Chile), which led to still more deaths attributable to capitalism.

Other capitalist despots include Mussolini, the Shah, Suharto, Orbán, Erdoğan, Putin, and plenty of others. *All* of them are responsible for numerous deaths.

Yes, many socialist leaders have made mistakes. So have communist leaders. But do capitalist authoritarians—and cruel or incompetent democratic leaders—get a pass just because they're capitalist?

"But there's no freedom under socialism!" we've been taught all our lives. "They ban books! They censor the media! They control what can be taught in schools!"

I forget. Are we talking about China or Florida?

Conservatives in the U.S. believe "leftists" have already taken away many of their rights, and those on the left feel the right-wing is committed to taking away ours. So do *any* of us here in "free" America feel free?

Patriots in the U.S. see America as the richest, best, most successful nation in the history of mankind. Yet there's almost nowhere in the entire country where a worker can afford a one-bedroom apartment on minimum wage. In most cities, there's no rent control, certainly no concept of housing as a human right.

Capitalism gives us hundreds of thousands of unhoused citizens in the *most successful capitalist* nation on the planet.

It begs the question—how do we define success?

Comparing life in a middle-class U.S. home to life in a Soviet gulag is as fair as comparing life in a U.S. federal prison to life in a three-bedroom apartment in Havana.

Capitalists in the U.S. and several other countries run for-profit prisons. Owners are incentivized to put more crimes on the books. Some judges accept bribes for convictions. Since the early 1990s, the U.S. has had one of the largest prison populations per capita in the world, peaking at 754 prisoners per 100,000 people in 2009. Even under the most extreme gulag period in the Soviet Union, their rate was comparable, between 714 and 892 per 100,000.

The U.S. is still one of the world's "leaders" when it comes to imprisoning our own people, with 20% of the world's prisoners in U.S. prisons, despite our citizens making up only 4.2% of the global population. We put our people in solitary confinement. We have Constitutionally legal prison slavery.

And let's remember that millions and millions of other prisoners around the world today sit mostly in prisons in capitalist countries, many for minor offenses. Poorhouses are even making a comeback in some nations.

Repressive rulers and oppressive laws are wrong, wherever they occur. An intellectually honest person can see that capitalists are committing plenty of atrocities against their own people every day.

Socialism doesn't need to be perfect to be better than capitalism. It's Harm Reduction.

That's not merely another term for "the lesser of two evils." Socialism as an ideology is sound, even if implementing it through imperfect people may be challenging. Capitalism, on the other hand, is exploitative by nature. And when you have an exploitative system run by imperfect people, you get...the misery we're currently experiencing.

There's no perfect healthcare system, but one economic system leaves more people behind than another. One has a higher literacy rate than another. One has better access to secondary education than another.

Scientists in developing countries were denied the formula to make vaccines against COVID or other diseases to save their citizens because for-profit pharmaceutical companies couldn't benefit from saving those lives. Over 21,000,000 people die from preventable and curable illnesses every year as a result, increasing capitalism's death toll significantly year after year.

In North America and Europe, grocery stores throw away 200 million tons of healthy food because it's not profitable to donate. They even sometimes pour bleach over the food to make sure no one else benefits, either. "If I can't have you, no one will!"

It almost sounds abusive.

Capitalists steal water from communities. They pollute groundwater for profit. They destroy soil for profit.

Every year, as the climate crisis worsens, we delay meaningful action so fossil fuel companies can earn billions more in profits. Capitalists try to convince us that only "market-based policies" can address the problem, but overwhelming evidence proves that this will *never* be the case.

Capitalism exploits people more than socialism. It kills more people than socialism. It will continue to wreak havoc on our environment until the planet can no longer sustain human life across huge swaths of its surface.

These aren't accidents caused by a few bad capitalists. Capitalism makes them inevitable.

Socialism might not solve all our problems. But it will solve some. Including many calamities *not* being addressed by the capitalism we've all been taught to worship as God's Celestial Finance System.

We can do better. We can accept that socialism will reduce harm to ourselves, our communities, and our planet. And we can do so without missionary zeal.

We can start by saying aloud the words that have been taboo most of our lives: Socialism is a valid alternative to capitalism.

We won't be struck by lightning.

And from here, we can begin learning at our own pace.

It's Time to Ration Fossil Fuels

Hot Tub Sales Plummet as Consumers Realize They Can Simply Wade in the Ocean Instead

Vegan Diets Soar as Climate-Driven Tick Disease Causes Allergic Reaction to Red Meat

Failing Electrical Grid Offers Texans Incentive to Learn Back-to-Stone-Age Skills

White Supremacy—the Popular New Color for Roof Shingles

We live in a world where it's difficult to tell the difference between a real headline and one from *Saturday Night Live*. Before long, even the most ridiculous headlines will become commonplace.

Insurance Companies Refuse to Insure Homeowners in Florida and California: "Those suckers are on their own!"

What do the many climate disasters we face almost daily have in common?

They *were* preventable at one time and now they're not.

No major party platform supports a ban on fracking, the bare minimum to begin stabilizing the climate. And no major party platform supports a ban on new fossil fuel projects. If we can't get by on the countless fossil fuel projects already in existence, there's no chance we'll slow global warming before we've reached multiple tipping points.

It's time to ration fossil fuels. We all knew this day would come, despite living in denial, but now that it's here, no one wants to do it. Businesses don't want to. Republicans don't want to. Democrats don't want to. Even climate scientists and climate activists don't *want* to do it.

Fossil fuel corporations don't want *anyone* to do it.

But it has to be done.

And just how exactly do we ration? Working out the particulars will require debate. Lots of it. Over months and years and multiple administrations. Meaning that by the time we start implementing those programs, even assuming we start those debates in Congress today, we'll still have passed multiple tipping points.

It's possible we're already too late. But pilots trying to save an out-of-control plane carrying 165 passengers keep fighting to the end. Sometimes, they crash anyway and everyone is killed. Other times, the crash kills all but a handful of passengers. But even those few survivors go on with their lives because the pilots didn't give up.

And sometimes, the pilots land safely despite overwhelming odds.

Any comprehensive approach to carbon rationing involves government regulation. Just as we can't expect the entire population to regulate their own food rationing during wartime or famine, limits must be imposed by a ruling body. People will always expect others to do the sacrificing. In wartime, we don't just "ask" people nicely to join the military. We draft. We require participation.

Is requiring citizens to defend their country "government overreach"?

In an emergency, only the government is powerful enough to coordinate resources and enforce laws and regulations to help the nation survive the emergency.

The global community can't quit fossil fuels overnight. Neither can a single nation, a city, or an individual.

What we *can* do, though, is ration.

Rationing fossil fuels, or carbon rationing, or whatever we choose to call it, won't simply mean everyone gets ten gallons of fuel a week. We need an even more comprehensive approach. Rationing fossil fuels will also require concrete steps to transition away from industrial agricultural farming. It will mean reducing beef and pork production.

Literal rationing of fossil fuel, of course, will undoubtedly be part of the program.

Each household is allotted so many gallons of gasoline a week. That can come in the form of credits we exchange at gas stations or that we hand to our uber driver. We'll input the credits when we conduct online orders so that delivery drivers have the fuel they need to drop off a package. If we run out of coupon numbers to input, then we get no more deliveries for the month.

In wartime, we convert factories that make cookware into factories that make ammunition. We convert automobile factories into factories that make planes or tanks or landing crafts.

We'll need to do the same thing in the war to stabilize the climate. We'll need electric instead of gas-powered vehicles. We'll need to produce more solar panels, more wind turbines, more batteries, more machinery to harness wave and thermal energy.

But we must also limit the number of personal vehicles—even electric vehicles—and produce more buses, light rail, trains, and high-speed trains. We keep our manufacturing jobs while transforming our nation to one that can function better with public transit, one that can perform at a high level while using fewer fossil fuels.

We'll be forced to focus more on public transit eventually. We're already behind many other nations on this front. We'll be left behind altogether as these adaptations become unavoidable. We can talk ourselves into believing that a 31-day streak of 110-degree weather is an anomaly, but when it lasts three months? Four? It simply won't be possible to ignore reality forever.

And there are countless other changes we'll need to make. We stop "allowing" work from home and start requiring more of it. We pay workers in fossil fuel industries to learn new skills. We hire those workers to develop and make technology to *store* solar, wind, and thermal energy.

We might even need Universal Basic Income as a stop gap measure until a new economy not centered around fossil fuels stabilizes along with the climate.

Disruptive? Stressful? Difficult?

Miserable?

Like World War II?

A war can't be won overnight. A famine isn't overcome in two weeks.

It will take time to adapt our fossil fuel-based culture to one that won't make a survivable climate impossible. But the alternative is to refuse to adapt.

Which means refusing to survive.

Yes, every one of these other options will require the use of varying amounts of fossil fuels. And every option will create its own waste and inflict its own damage on the environment. Short of eliminating all human activity on the planet, we'll always have an impact.

But there are degrees of damage. Some damage is survivable and some isn't.

No one likes rationing during wartime.

Only idiots and sadists like war.

No one likes rationing during a famine.

But most people like surviving famine and war.

Housing Market Opens Up after 60K Homeowners Die in European Heatwave

Republican County Shifts Blue after Rural Town of 20,000 Obliterated in Wildfire

Democratic Party in Peril as Voters Demand Action over Promises

Which headline will we see next?

Rationing fossil fuels won't be fun, but neither will 110-degree summers in New York, Chicago, and Seattle. Or 120-degree summers in New Orleans and Miami and Houston.

Let's choose rationing, which means choosing to at least *try* surviving climate change.

And maybe one day we'll read a victorious headline:

VE-Day—It's All Over

President Truman Declares Today as V-J Day

Civilization Saved from Climate Disaster in the Nick of Time!

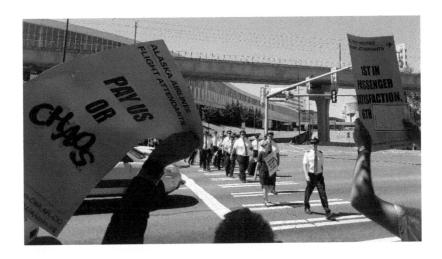

Rally for flight attendants at Sea-Tac airport.

Make Hoarding Wealth Illegal

We all know hoarders, those poor, afflicted souls who can't stop themselves from buying and storing more things than they could ever use in a lifetime. Clothes and plates and trinkets and unopened boxes and any number of other items are piled everywhere in their home, a tiny path left for the hoarder to navigate from their chair to the kitchen to the bathroom and back. Sometimes, even their bed is covered with so many items it's now unusable.

We feel pity for these people, perhaps repulsion. But we understand it's a mental illness of some sort. They truly can't help themselves. And, unless their home is a fire hazard right next door to ours, it's mostly their personal problem.

But hoarding is different if there's a famine. When there's not enough food to go around and people are literally starving to death, it's not just a personal matter if our neighbor's home is crammed to the ceiling with canned goods and produce. They have more than they could ever eat in twenty years, and our family might very well die if our neighbor refuses to share.

Did our neighbor buy that food with his or her own money? Is it legally theirs? What claim do *we* have over someone else's food?

Well, laws change during a crisis. It becomes illegal to hoard, even if you're using your own money.

In wartime, when food is scarce, the government issues ration cards. Everyone gets just so much. Perhaps people make counterfeit ration cards or sell real cards on the black market, but there's some sense of community obligation. The only way to get through the crisis is to take on a shared burden. We all suffer a little so everyone has a chance to survive.

That's the case in wartime. It's the case during a famine.

And it needs to be the case during late-stage capitalism. With half a million unhoused people in the country, with millions more living in substandard, unsafe conditions, we have ultrarich hoarders with two, three, seven or more personal homes. We have hoarders who own hundreds or thousands of rental properties, gouging renters with ever higher rent.

We have the superrich who can afford the best healthcare in the world while tens of millions of their neighbors go without even minimal care.

Are the superrich using their own money to buy those homes and pay for their doctors? That's debatable, given the exploitation necessary to accumulate vast wealth. But even if legally that money is theirs, we're in a crisis, with people dying for lack of the basics, and hoarding wealth can no longer be tolerated.

The top 1% in the U.S. own 32% of the wealth while the bottom 50% own a mere 2.6%.

We've been taught that those smart enough and strong enough to hoard power and wealth deserve their treasure. It's human nature. It's evolution itself. The survival of the fittest.

But who has taught us that?

Why, it's those with power and wealth.

What possible motivation could they have for teaching such a doctrine?

One person owns so much wealth he can afford to build a personal rocketship to take him into space, while another person working three jobs can't even afford a car to get to work in.

Imagine extreme weather conditions—drought, hailstorms, flooding, derechos—destroy so many crops that next year we face a famine. Our neighbor is industrious and rich and planned ahead. He's got lots of food, and he paid for it with his hard-earned money. He bought it before the famine even began.

Is it fair to now consider him a criminal simply for having foresight? For keeping what's rightfully his?

We're unhappy with the situation, but fair is fair, we think. That's not *our* food.

As we begin to grow hungry, we learn that our neighbor has hoarded so many provisions he could eat six huge meals a day, every day for four hundred years, and *still* barely make a dent in his food supply.

Yet he keeps hoarding *more* food even as the famine worsens so that despite eating those six huge meals a day, his hoard keeps growing *larger* as his neighbors start to die off.

He's got so much fresh produce it's literally rotting before he can eat it all. But he insists on waiting until it rots and then throwing it away rather than share. He isn't benefitting in any way from keeping that food, *can't* use it, but *still* refuses to alleviate our hunger.

How do we feel about our neighbor now?

Does it matter if his actions are guided by mental illness? Addiction? Compulsive behavior? Selfishness?

It's the impact that counts, not the reason behind it.

We ask our neighbor politely to share and he brushes us off.

We ask again, still politely. Then we demand.

But our neighbor has so much wealth and power hoarded along with his food that he can afford guards to protect him and his food storage. He can bribe politicians to create exemptions for him in the law code.

He's not going to give away so much as one ounce of bread. Why, with scientific advances, he just might live four hundred years. He's going to need all that food for himself. This famine might last a very long time.

At what point does our concept of fairness change?

Hoarding wealth is no different, when that money is needed by tens of millions of our neighbors for food, housing, medicine, and everything else that makes life both survivable and bearable.

In a drought, we criminalize watering lawns and washing cars. If a superrich neighbor with ten cars wants to wash all of them while watering his expansive lawn, and smugly tells us he can afford the water bill *and* the fines, is that okay? Even if *we* end up not having water to flush our toilets, wash our clothes, grow our food, or simply drink enough to stay alive?

We create the laws. *We* create the social contract. *We* decide how food and housing and wealth is distributed.

We need to change our mindset, recognize we've been programmed—brainwashed—to accept that hoarding wealth is not only natural but good, because such a belief serves those who hoard at our expense.

Once we realize this truth, we can start taking measures to ensure that all of us have a fighting chance to survive in a world increasingly full of war, famine, drought, and other climate disasters, many of which, of course, are caused by the hoarders themselves.

Moral Superiority Doesn't Pay the Bills, Money Does, So Tax the Rich

If we think it's morally wrong to take money from the rich to pay for society's infrastructure, it's quite possible we're right.

I wonder, though, why if taking money from someone rich through taxation is wrong, it's somehow morally right to take it from the poor and middle class. Either way, we're taking money away from people who have earned it. Why is it morally right to take it from the poorer folks but sinful to take it from richer ones? What makes the rich morally exempt from proportional responsibility?

In the end, I'm not sure it matters what's morally right regarding taxation. The reality is that infrastructure costs money. Taxation is a matter of practicality, not a method of moral instruction. If we want a functioning society, we must fund it, and the funds can only come from those who have it.

If you want to bottle water, do you set up your bottling plant in a region with lakes, springs, and aquifers, or do you move to the desert?

It may be a morally superior decision to tax people with less money so that those with more can "invest" and "create jobs," but it's not a fiscally sound one. Morality won't get us a functioning society. Poorer folks are simply unable to fund one, no matter how much we or they or anyone may want them to.

If a mugger demands your money but you aren't carrying your wallet, no amount of coercion will make that wallet magically appear, no amount of willingness to cooperate will produce a billfold out of thin air.

If we want funds to develop and sustain a functioning infrastructure, should we fine homeless folks or should we tax people who have money?

If poor people are responsible for their poverty, if homeless people are weak, morally bankrupt losers who deserve to be treated with disdain, if working class folks struggling to pay their bills should have forced themselves to develop more skills and gotten better jobs, fine. We can judge these "losers" all we want. But judging them, punishing them, being repulsed by them, ignoring them—none of that changes their account balances. They still don't have the funds to build roads, pay police and firefighter salaries, or do any of the other things that will prevent our cities from falling into ruin.

You don't get a blood donation *from* someone who's bleeding out.

Locals in Seattle don't stroll through Pike Place Market anymore. They don't shop in Pioneer Square or in the downtown corridor. When they come out of the light rail station on 3rd Avenue, they see dozens of homeless people camped out across the street. Businesses are boarded up.

In Columbia City, in Mount Baker, in neighborhood after neighborhood, store windows are bashed in, there's graffiti everywhere, trash wherever we walk, tents and RVs and vans where people make their homes next to burned out, abandoned stores.

And all this takes place while high rise after high rise is constructed throughout the city, beautiful new buildings next door to homeless encampments and lots filled with "tiny houses."

Income inequality, income disparity, the wealth gap—whatever we want to call it—has created not only a tale of two cities but a tale of two nations. And when one nation preys on another, when there's an effectual apartheid, the inevitable outcome is always disastrous.

"No Justice, No Peace" isn't a threat. It's a statement of fact.

If you want to relax, do you go to a park filled with flowers and trees or do you go to a park filled with homeless encampments?

If you want misery, where do you go?

The "where" is policy. If we want to live in a safe, beautiful city and a safe, beautiful country, we need to enact policies that will get us there.

"Let's crack down on crime!"

We already conduct homeless sweeps. We already bust unions. We've already built more and larger prisons. We've already given tax refunds to the wealthiest among us. We've already given tax breaks to corporations. We already subsidize many of the richest corporations.

Where has that gotten us?

To dystopia.

Insanity is doing the same thing over and over and expecting different results.

Some feel that spending cuts and "tightening our belts" is the solution. Some want to defund public transit, defund public schools, defund public libraries. Making everyone fend for themselves, they insist, will save the city, state, and nation money while simultaneously forcing people to improve their moral character.

But we don't have to guess the outcome. This isn't a theoretical question. We've *seen* the results of such actions again and again. Every act of austerity only exacerbates the problem.

Now we have folks who can't get to work in a timely manner. They lose their jobs. They end up receiving unemployment.

If we defund unemployment programs, these folks simply become homeless. We haven't resolved any problems. We're only worsened the dystopia. We see it happening right before our eyes.

Where will we go if we bust more unions, build more prisons, give more tax breaks to the wealthy? Will that somehow create water in the desert?

Will it magically force the poorest among us to produce the funds necessary to create a functioning infrastructure, like a mugger demanding a wallet we don't have? Even a professional magician can't *really* pull a rabbit out of a hat unless that rabbit is already there.

Income inequality isn't alchemy.

For those who demand "reform" of capitalism, the same questions apply. If we want justice and equity, do we keep promoting the system that *creates* these problems, that pits groups against one another, that *depends* on these problems to survive?

Or do we go somewhere else?

We worry that if our city demands corporations and the wealthy pay their fair share of taxes then those businesses or residents will move outside city limits.

We worry that if our state demands corporations and the wealthy pay their fair share of taxes, those businesses and wealthy residents will move out of state.

We worry that if our nation demands corporations and the wealthy pay their fair share of taxes, those businesses and wealthy citizens will move out of the country.

But what we're really acknowledging is that capitalism is blackmail and by its very nature can never provide an adequate infrastructure for the people of a city, state, or nation, no matter how rich that nation is.

Under capitalism, a handful of wealthy people will always hoard money at the expense of others. It's the principal feature of capitalism, not a bug.

This inequity is propped up by the belief that those with more money are morally, intellectually, and spiritually superior to those with less.

And so what if that's true?

It doesn't matter if the superiority we feel is for our ethnicity, our religion, our education, our intelligence, our political ideology, or anything else. Our being superior still doesn't alter economic reality.

We can only get money to keep our society functioning—and have that society be a place we'd actually want to live—from those who have the money. That's true no matter how desperately we wish it were otherwise, no matter how superior we may be.

A functioning society isn't free.

Justice and equity aren't free.

Even freedom isn't free.

But just as a drug addict will keep using while his marriage and friendships crumble, as her performance at work deteriorates, as his whole world collapses around him, so we keep supporting politicians who funnel money to those at the top, even as our society falls apart.

When an alcoholic hits rock bottom, he may end up on skid row.

What happens when a nation hits rock bottom?

That's not a theoretical question, either. We've seen what happens when income disparity becomes too great.

But there *is* a solution.

We peasants learn to accept our moral inferiority and continue to allow the wealthiest among us to hoard their money, and everything will turn out just fine.

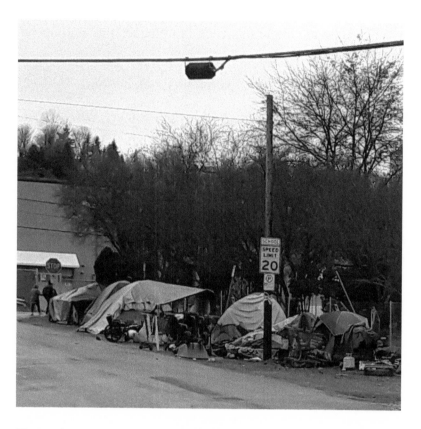

Tents in a Seattle school zone.

Capricious Allies Aren't Allies

Capricious allies aren't allies.

Fickle support isn't support.

Recently, I had an uncomfortable discussion with a close friend. "Did you see the news?" Toby asked. "Protesters blocked the street near the light rail station in the U District for an *hour!*" He shook his head. "I don't care what you're protesting," he went on. "Once you do something that infantile, you've lost all support for your cause."

"They were protesting genocide in Gaza," I said. "Didn't you say last week you were against genocide?"

"Yes!" Toby glared into the distance somewhere over my shoulder.

"But not now?"

Toby nodded.

I was confused. "So…it's the *form* of protest you protest?" I asked.

Toby nodded again.

I still wasn't sure I understood. After all, what he was saying didn't really make sense. I must have been missing something. "You said you signed a petition asking Biden to stop arming Israel?"

"Sure did."

"You emailed your representatives and senators?"

"Obviously."

"You called your representatives and senators on the phone and demanded a ceasefire?"

"Yep."

"And for ending the occupation?"

"Of *course* I did. I told you I used to be against genocide."

"But when protesters blocked the street, that changed your mind?"

"You bet it did!" Toby glared again. "Now I don't care if the Israeli military kills another 25,000 civilians. They can keep killing babies, blowing up schools and hospitals. They can keep starving everyone. They can keep cutting off water and electricity." Toby's jaw was clenched so tightly he could barely get the words out. "They can kill all two million people in Gaza for all I care!" He stopped to catch his breath. "I mean, those protesters blocked *streets*, for God's sake!"

I wondered if I was being secretly filmed for an episode of *Pranked*. My friend's position simply didn't seem possible.

"Do you feel the same way about *any* cause people are protesting?" I asked. "Do you support reproductive rights?"

"I *did*," Toby admitted, "until pro-choice protesters blocked Third Avenue. *Now* I think anyone who gets an abortion or provides assistance should be arrested. Maybe executed for murder."

My mouth fell open.

"Blocking streets is *bad*!" Toby took a deep breath. "It's *rude*!"

"So you don't support efforts to mitigate climate change, either?"

"Once protesters cause even the slightest inconvenience, they prove how selfish they are. How can I support selfish people? How can *you*?"

My friend Toby was my age, in his mid-sixties, so I quickly thought back to the many street protests I'd seen or participated in over the decades.

"Did you support AIDS research?"

"Until ACT UP started acting up."

"Did you support investigating clergy abuse?" I asked.

"Until Sinead O'Connor tore up a picture of the Pope."

I still thought my friend might be fucking with me, but he'd literally stopped fucking me in the middle of our first date, changing his mind and going home instead. I knew him to flit arbitrarily from idea to idea on many occasions.

But on issues this serious?

"Are you against police brutality?" I asked.

"Not anymore! Protesters caused a *lot* of people a *lot* of inconvenience."

"Are you even for LGBTQ rights?"

"After all the furor they've caused over the years! Please."

"But you're gay yourself!"

Toby shook his head and sniffed. "It's the principle."

While it's hopefully clear by now that "Toby" isn't a real person, we all know people who make similarly ridiculous claims. I have friends who refuse to participate in or show support for any kind of "disruptive" protest. "It causes a backlash," they say. "It does more harm than good."

What does harm is allowing injustice to continue unchallenged.

I'm not sure we need to worry about the fickle support of anyone who is 100% against the slaughter of innocents until they see protesters block an intersection for half an hour.

With friends like these…

Or better, with commitment and dedication like this…

These are not people we need to take advice from on Best Protest Strategies. Or probably much of anything else. Fickle determination isn't an oxymoron because the only part of the term that's accurate is "fickle," and that part is 100% precise.

When anyone tells me that Action A, B, or C is the wrong way to change policy, I tell them, "If you know the right way to get governments to stop war or provide universal healthcare or stabilize the climate, why in God's name aren't you doing it?"

The reason isn't because they're lazy or lack commitment. It's because there isn't a perfect solution, a perfect act of protest. We're all just doing the best we can to right wrongs and make the world a better place.

Well, all of us except those who tell us to stop bothering people.

Whether blocking streets or throwing soup or toppling statues or any other disruptive act is the "best" method of protest can always be debated. But inconveniencing others is hardly a justification for avoiding a particular strategy. Doing so is inevitable. And necessary. Change won't happen without it.

So let's stop worrying about offending folks and keep doing whatever we must to bring about the positive change we desperately need.

Sleeping on light rail when there's nowhere else.

Act as if Acting Matters

If you have an extra $4653 lying around, you can purchase a sacred relic—part of the suit Donald Trump wore when he was arrested. For the fourth time.

If you don't have quite that much spare change, you can still hire expelled congressperson George Santos for a mere $500 to film a short message of support for you or a loved one.

Perhaps you can donate to Joe Biden's re-election campaign in the hope that throwing money at an unpopular candidate will stop people from remembering how he betrayed rail workers, failed to forgive student loan debt, promoted the expansion of fossil fuel projects, and supported the slaughter of innocents in Gaza.

Unfortunately, there's no end to the ridiculous in our everyday lives. The same species that can build space stations also includes members who think vaccinating a dog against rabies will give it autism. How can we expect to rally the cooperation necessary to address homelessness or any other issue when we have groups that believe MH370 disappeared after being sucked through a wormhole over the Indian Ocean?

Let's champion thinking in a time of thoughtlessness.

Of course, even rational people have difficulty knowing how to tackle the multitude of problems we're facing. There's rising fascism around the world, wars and civil wars, human rights abuses here and abroad, the collapse of late-stage capitalism, and an ever-accelerating climate crisis.

All these problems need to be addressed immediately. So just where do we begin?

Politicians who don't want to pass better laws or policies will always find a way to deflect. **We must stop allowing them to blackmail us into inaction**.

Naysayers are quick to point out what *won't* work when pressuring lawmakers and yet never seem to have an answer as to what *will*. If they do know the answer, they clearly haven't acted on it, because none of these problems has yet been solved.

All they're sure of is that what *we're* doing is wrong.

If an athlete protests racism by taking a knee, we hear, "That's not the right place for a protest." If she rallies in front of a stadium, "She's being disruptive." If he throws a rock through a window, "He should protest peacefully."

If a parent protests the lack of background checks after a man with a history of violence buys a gun and shoots up a school, "Now is not the time" to talk about regulations. If we wait for the one week a year when there are no mass shootings, assuming there is one, there's some other excuse.

Far too often, the resistance to action comes from those who fully understand we have serious problems to solve. They're simply more worried about "optics."

"Oh, if you block traffic, you'll turn people against you."

Is a human rights advocate who has charged that killing civilians and children in Gaza is an atrocity really going to complain about such an inconvenience? "I was all for ending mass murder, but if you're going to make me fifteen minutes late for work, then fuck it, go ahead and slaughter another 20,000 people right now!"

Yet we hear this kind of "reasoning" in response to every proposed action.

"Oh, if you throw a can of soup against the glass protecting a painting, you'll just make things worse."

Are there *really* folks who want to speed up a transition to renewables who are going to say, "I was all for mitigating the sixth mass extinction event, but if you're going to be rude inside a museum, then by golly, burn the planet to a crisp and every human on it!"

If blocking traffic or taking a knee or gluing our hands to a picture frame or chaining ourselves to a pipeline really does end someone's support for a cause, it's clear their support wasn't terribly strong to begin with. Did we really lose an ally?

Worse, if "supporters" are so easily manipulated, so driven by emotion, that they can no longer grasp logic, there's little hope we'll pull together and do what must be done to address any of these problems in a meaningful way.

So what's a thinking, feeling person to do?

For one, we don't give in to blackmail.

The only way to move forward on climate or any issue worth fighting for is to **act as if acting matters**. If acting *doesn't* matter, if every act of protest is counterproductive, we've lost whether we act or not.

But if acting *does* matter, and we've allowed ourselves to be blackmailed into not acting out of fear of "making things worse if we upset people," then we've lost when we didn't need to.

Progress, human rights, and societal advancement are never givens. Time alone solves nothing. There's no guarantee that if we fight, we'll win. The only sure thing is that if we don't fight, we'll certainly lose.

Giving up is a choice. Let's make a better one.

So for God's sake—or, better yet, humanity's—let's choose to act.

Seattle homeless encampment in the rain.

Climate Change Is a Pyroclastic Flow Rushing Toward Us

"Closing my shop and moving to another city costs way too much. I'm barely getting by as it is. I'll just stay here, keep working my butt off as usual, and hope for the best."

Some shopkeeper in Pompeii

The rumblings were there, the earthquakes, the plumes of smoke and gas. Some residents heeded the warnings and left. The others, perhaps too ignorant to understand the signs, rationalized them away.

Not everyone who stayed was incinerated, of course. Some found refuge in underground bunkers...where they slowly suffocated to death.

Will transitioning quickly away from fossil fuels negatively impact our economy?

That's the wrong question. It's like asking, "Will I need rehab after a serious stroke?" or "Will buying a house cost money?"

Why ask questions with foregone conclusions?

A better question is, "How will we die if we don't transition quickly away from fossil fuels?"

Here are a few other questions we might ask ourselves:

1. Will we lose our home to a wildfire?

2. Will we lose our farm, our livestock, our pets to a wildfire?

3. Will we lose our crops to a drought?

4. Will we lose our crops to a flood or a derecho?

5. Will our grocery bill go up because someone *else* lost their crops and livestock?

6. Will we go hungry? Will there be a famine? Will our family starve to death?

7. Are we okay with *other* people starving to death as long as we're not inconvenienced?

8. How reliable is our electric grid in the face of severe heat waves?

9. How high will sea level rise? And how quickly? How will that impact the property I hope to leave my children?

10. What happens when millions of people are displaced by the changing climate? Where will they go? How will that impact neighboring countries? *Our* country? The global economy? My 401k?

We see rather quickly that these aren't isolated questions. They compound, like interest. And they're not either/or. We don't simply ask ourselves if *either* scenario 2 will play out *or* if scenario 5 will. All these scenarios and more are already taking place on a larger and larger scale every year. And they'll only get worse.

Vesuvius will do more than loom over us. It will explode. That part isn't in question. The question is what we're going to do about it.

Worry about the inconvenience? Pretend that pyroclastic flows aren't real?

If individual residents of Pompeii want to ignore reality, that's on them. Like Harry R. Truman, the lodgekeeper who chose certain death rather than leave his home near Mount St. Helens. The 28,000 residents of Saint-Pierre who ignored the geological warnings on the island of Martinique didn't fare so well, either.

But presidents and senators and members of parliament and prime ministers need to do more than live in luxury off the taxes wrung from the shopkeepers of Pompeii.

You can't extract additional taxes from folks who refused to leave.

"My beautiful mosaic will be damaged if I try to relocate it."

Pompeii resident found curled up next to his dog

"I've got the best corner in town for selling clams."

Pompeii resident found along the shore beside twenty-seven other bodies

"The view from my window is to die for."

Pompeii resident found crouched over an infant

We can certainly try to make our transition away from fossil fuels as painless as possible. But whether that transition is easy or difficult or somewhere in between, it'll still be impossible to avoid. The magma is rising quickly.

The only questions left to ask are whether we'll start to run *before* or *after* the pyroclastic flow slams against our front door.

And just where we expect to go.

23 degrees outside, 70 degrees on the bus.

Power in Solidarity for Seattle Workers

A few weeks ago, the Coalition of City Unions walked out of a contract bargaining meeting with City of Seattle officials when the City's counteroffer to their original 1% COLA was…a 1% COLA.

The Cost-of-Living-Adjustment isn't the only issue holding up the contract. Unions making up 6000 City workers are also negotiating market rate wage adjustments, up to 10% for some job classifications. In addition, we're fighting better boot and clothing allowances in some departments, faster vacation accrual, changes to our discipline and safety practices, adjustments for outdoor work during heatwaves and wildfire smoke, and more flexibility in our Alternative Work Arrangements.

And honestly, for a good bit more. The previous contract failed us in many ways.

City officials were so shocked when coalition team members walked out of bargaining that at the next bargaining session, Mayor Bruce Harrell showed up in person. The new COLA offer was 2.37%, the first movement in over a year but still a huge cut in pay for workers, given the 16% inflation over the previous few years.

The bargaining team rejected the offer.

Mayor Harrell said he'd spoken with the mayor of Los Angeles, who'd recently faced a one-day strike by workers there. Harrell seemed shaken, according to several union reps present at the bargaining session.

But when Coalition members said that unless the City came up with a fair contract before September 19, we were going to rally at City Hall, Mayor Harrell told them to go ahead and "rally your asses off!"

He insisted, according to several folks present, that the rally wouldn't affect him *or* the bargaining.

City officials then offered one of the eleven unions in the coalition two different packages. If the union agreed to break away from the coalition, they'd be given 5% more than if they stayed with the coalition.

They stayed with the coalition.

At the next bargaining session, every union leader spoke up against this divide-and-conquer attempt, committing publicly to each other and to City officials that they would continue to work in solidarity for a fair contract for all. Such a demonstration had never occurred before during contract negotiations, for this or previous contracts.

City leaders admitted they weren't prepared with a counteroffer and had to cancel bargaining for the day.

City officials and union leaders are now meeting weekly, but there is still little movement. City negotiators hint at possible layoffs if they're forced to pay a higher COLA, but 65% of City workers aren't even paid through the General

Fund. And with an ideology of austerity, the City can order layoffs regardless of any concessions union members make.

We're not fighting for what we *want*, after all. We're fighting for what we *need*.

The Tacoma Housing Authority a few miles south of us just raised the minimum wage for its workers to $32 an hour because they discovered too many of their own employees were contacting them for housing assistance. The cost of living in the region has skyrocketed over the past few years. Rent costs even more in Seattle, one of the most expensive cities in the nation.

Student loan payments are starting up again, another drain on worker paychecks.

Over 700 City workers have committed to joining the rally at City Hall on September 19 and are encouraging their coworkers to join in. Some of those hesitant to attend are nervous, confusing rallying with striking.

But we rally in hopes of avoiding a strike.

"If you think 1% is fair and you're okay with that," some workers suggest, "then don't come to the rally."

It's not that different from what my dentist tells me. "Floss only those teeth you want to keep."

No one gives up power (or money) voluntarily. We must show up at the rally and give City officials undeniable evidence we're united in the fight for a fair contract.

We're asking City workers to arrange for the day off, or for half the day off, or to cover a shift for another worker who needs the day off to participate. We're asking folks to carpool, provide babysitting, do whatever we need to help each other make a difference together.

More than that, we're asking community members to come to the rally to show City leaders that this is important to them, too. We want preachers, rabbis, imams, and priests to come to City Hall on September 19.

We want members of other unions to come to City Hall in solidarity.

We want *you* to come to City Hall. Please, invite your bowling league, your bridge club, your quilting group. Ask your yoga pals, your tennis partners, your friends at the food bank, your gym buddies.

Make a TikTok in support of a fair contract. Share it with your friends across the country. We want nationwide attention, too.

Every body counts. If you can come in person to Seattle City Hall on Tuesday, September 19, from 3:30 to 5:00, please come and use your presence to win workers a fair contract.

Cruelty by Proxy Is Still Cruel

"I don't let politics get in the way of my friendships," a Mormon family member told me. Her tone implied I was being unreasonable, a fanatic, for taking issue with her voting—twice—for Donald Trump.

But if A=B and B=C, then A=C.

The transitive property is why I can no longer maintain a relationship with many of my Latter-day Saint family members and former missionary colleagues.

You can't vote for people who oppress others without sharing a significant portion of the responsibility for that oppression, especially when the candidates campaign on *promises* of oppression.

If you donate to political organizations whose *goals* are to deny healthcare or education or housing to tens of millions of your fellow citizens, then you're more than just tangentially responsible for the suffering of those tens of millions.

You can't financially support people who deny the reality of climate change without accepting your part in the destruction of farms, towns, and communities across the planet.

"Well, I don't even like some of the Republicans I vote for," this family member told me, "but Democrats are worse."

But to believe that a rainbow flag constitutes sexual abuse is delusional. To believe that high school students who have survived a mass shooting are too young to handle learning about slavery is beyond delusional.

At best, these beliefs reveal that your values about what constitutes kindness and compassion are vastly different from mine.

"Tough love" which demands that people with diabetes lose limbs because they can't afford the care they need is "easy disregard."

It's not something I can gloss over.

The truth is, I find it difficult to maintain relationships with folks who sing Joe Biden's praise at every opportunity, too. "Look at all he's done to save the climate in his Inflation Reduction Act!"

What I see is that he's opened more public land to drilling than any president in history, when the results of such a decision are clearer now than they've ever been.

But this divisiveness over politics and religion is tiresome, distasteful. The animosity is destroying our country. Can't we all just get along?

Only if your personal beliefs stay personal.

"Mormons are so nice," I've often heard people say over the years. But to smile and bring over a plate of cookies while working to make my existence a criminal offense is rather a mixed bag, isn't it? I'll gladly forego the cookies in exchange for humane treatment.

If you pay tithing to a church that oppresses LGBTQ people who aren't even followers of your religion, you're still hurting me, my friends, and my chosen family, no matter who you vote for.

That's not okay.

Mormons are fine with shunning "apostates" but feel offended if *we* do the shunning because of *their* bad behavior.

Many of my LDS family and former friends regularly post their support of elected officials who openly attack democracy, promote stochastic terrorism, and foment civil war.

"No politician is perfect" just isn't going to cut it as a defense.

The family member who insisted she never let politics interfere in her friendships seemed shocked when I turned down her generous offer to associate with me despite my decadence. Didn't I understand the favor she was granting?

After all, *she'd* never do anything to hurt me.

If a proxy baptism is valid, so is proxy cruelty.

Given the gravity of the escalating climate crisis, voting for corporate Democrats is also a vote against humanity.

That's a problem, too. There's plenty of proxy sin to go around.

Lesser evils are still evil.

If the words "nice" and "love" and "righteous" are to have any meaning at all, they must include alleviating misery, not crushing people we hate.

We heal the sick. We feed the hungry. We welcome the outcasts and immigrants.

All those "woke" things Jesus did.

Unfortunately, that glow in the east isn't the Messiah returning. It's another wildfire.

My hope is that enough of us of all faiths finally recognize the need to move away from the cruel capitalism championed by both Republicans and Democrats before that decision is made for us, not by the Second Coming but by the Sixth Mass Extinction.

Let's be kind to one another. And to ourselves. It's what any politician worth voting for would demand. And what any god worth following would want.

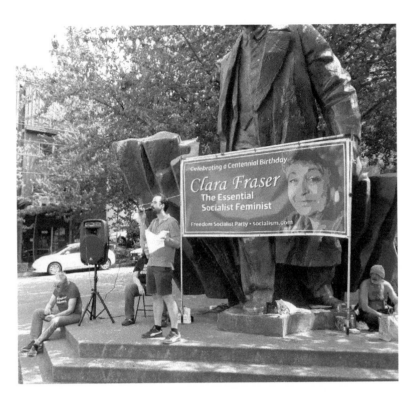

July 4th rally at Lenin statue in Seattle.

Elderly Are Disproportionately Impacted by Climate Change and Should Sue Those Responsible

The recent victory in Montana (*Held v. Montana*) by a group of young people suing the state for promoting fossil fuels was a surprise. The ruling will almost certainly be appealed, but even if it turns out to be only a partial victory, it's worth celebrating. And amplifying.

I'm sixty-two, my husband is seventy, and the other day, a sixty-eight-year-old friend commenting on the case asked, "Why can't old people sue?"

So far, most of the bodies identified in the Lahaina wildfire were elderly, too slow to escape the flames. Many of the hundreds of people in the U.S. who die of heatstroke every year are elderly. Many of the thousands who die in Europe from prolonged heatwaves are elderly.

We have a right to live to a ripe old age. If you break into someone's home and murder a ninety-five-year-old woman, it's still murder, isn't it? Even if the woman might have died naturally six months later. Six months of life matter. So do six years. Or twenty years.

Many people in their sixties are dying from the impacts of global warming. The decades of life we're being deprived of matter. People our age can still work productively and contribute to society. We can write books and songs and movies. We teach. We're smart enough to invent things. We babysit our grandchildren.

But even if we weren't "productive," we *still* matter. And we certainly don't deserve to die in flash floods that wash us away along with our homes. Gasping for breath in 115-degree weather without air conditioning.

Trapped in our beds as wildfires race toward us. Is that the kind of death *you'd* choose for yourself?

The fossil fuel industry and the politicians they buy are powerful. If we're to have any chance at saving ourselves, we must tackle the crisis from as many angles as possible. Protests, rallies, activists blocking streets or gluing themselves to picture frames are all part of the cumulative effort we must make.

Youth demanding a right to a stable climate is essential.

And elderly people insisting they have a right to a full lifespan.

What about an ADA-related case showing how climate change impacts people with disabilities?

Or a case with farmers as plaintiffs showing how their businesses are being destroyed by drought?

Perhaps fishers who lose a billion shellfish during a heatwave?

Tourist industries in places it's now too hot to visit for longer periods each year?

Earthjustice, can you put together a case? How about you, Sierra Club? We don't want only a single organization to work on this. Perhaps Greenpeace can make one case while Climate Action Network makes another. Friends of the Earth can produce one legal challenge while 350.org produces a different one.

And we don't just sue county or state governments. We can sue companies or entire industries, the way plaintiffs have sued tobacco and gun manufacturers.

Screenwriters can write new versions of *Runaway Jury* to help audiences understand the stakes.

We have dozens if not hundreds of opportunities. And when the groups destroying a survivable climate are so powerful, we'll need to take advantage of every one.

Just as workers need solidarity across sectors to advance the welfare of all workers, climate activists in different organizations with different specific goals need to support each other as we all work together for a sustainable climate.

Old people who are often cast aside have decades of experience fighting battles. Let's use that knowledge to help young people. And the disabled and farmers and fishers. And ourselves.

Because climate breakdown hurts everyone. And we all have a right to fight for our lives.

Do Not Go Gently into That Gas Chamber

Okay, let's get the requisite Godwin's Law analogy out of the way. Fighting the fossil fuel industry is like fighting Nazis in a global war.

Nazis are powerful and brutal and scary. Many people in the 1930s and '40s gave up without a fight. Many who did fight were crushed.

How many of us have watched a Holocaust movie and thought, "If *I'd* been there, I would have…"

We'd have been like the gentile wives who demanded their Jewish husbands be released from Rosenstrasse.

We'd have been like the saboteurs who brought down a heavy water lab in Norway.

We'd have been like Raoul Wallenberg, forging passports for Jews fleeing occupied Hungary.

Backseat driving, Monday morning quarterbacking, and pontificating proudly about our bravery is easy when we don't currently need to display any of our own.

The thing is, we *do* need to act courageously because there *is* evil to fight—the fossil fuel industry leading the entire human species to the greenhouse gas chambers.

Most of us have long been aware of the disaster that is climate breakdown and have called our representatives. We've signed petitions, sent emails. We've waved protest signs at rallies, demanded our universities and banks divest from fossil fuels. We make sacrifices to lessen our personal impact on the environment.

And yet.

Despite minimal progress made over the past decades—solar panels, electric cars, wind turbines—every year, we still pump out more greenhouse gases than ever before. And there's no end in sight. There's plenty of vague *talk* about an end but those "details" are little more than hot gas.

So why *don't* we fight fossil fuel Nazis? Is it because we don't really think the climate emergency will get as bad as predicted? Perhaps we feel that to fight effectively, we need more money than we have, more expertise. Maybe we hope to be one of the survivors if we can just manage to stay out of trouble until everything blows over.

Some who warn against "extreme" action tell us that the far right will use any damage we might do as an excuse to come down hard against activists, against the left, against democracy itself. Our actions might make things worse.

But what's worse than accelerating the sixth mass extinction event we've already started? What's worse than missing the 1.5° C goal? And the 2.0° C goal? And the 3.5° C goal?

Will the stakes *ever* be high enough to warrant more than asking nicely for people not to kill us?

In just the one year between 2022 and 2023, the United Nations Office for the Coordination of Humanitarian Affairs reported a 60% increase in the number of deaths from landslides, a 278% increase in the number of people killed in wildfires, and a whopping 340% increase in deaths resulting from storms.

The World Health Organization estimates that by 2030, global warming will cause over a quarter of a million additional deaths each year. Not counting those killed in wars over oil. Yet we're not allowed to so much as throw an egg against the door of a fossil fuel company? Key the side of a fossil fuel exec's car?

For almost any situation we find ourselves in today, there's a Holocaust equivalent, so let's find an analogy that speaks to us and will push us collectively and as individuals to action.

Perhaps we have a decent amount of money and social standing. We don't want to risk that. And besides, that money and standing might get us past the round ups when others are deported. So we hold back on rocking the boat.

But there's a reason we're still finding stolen artwork confiscated from the wealthiest Jews eighty years ago and returning it to their surviving relatives.

Perhaps we're so assimilated we feel immune to disaster. Maybe we're part of the fossil fuel industry ourselves or are executives in other businesses dependent on fossil fuels.

Should we ask assimilated gay Ernst Röhm if being an integral part of the Nazi machinery protected him? Shall we ask the assimilated Jews of Berlin how they fared in the camps? Or the Catholic nun of Jewish descent who died along with them?

Maybe we're so financially strapped we've become collaborators, knowing we're wrong but not sure what else we can do besides cooperate. Perhaps a few of us rationalize being war profiteers. If we can earn money, even by supporting pro-fossil fuel candidates, we can donate that money to good causes.

There will always be a justification for looking the other way.

Perhaps, though, we're already eco-activists, partisans hiding in the forest, the French resistance, righteous gentiles hiding Jews. We're the von Trapp family leaving all our wealth behind rather than support an evil regime.

Are we the partisans who bombed railroads and bridges and ammunition depots? Are we the resistance who made assassination attempts?

Do we know what happened to the Jews who tried to commit these serious crimes?

Do we know what happened to the Jews who *didn't* fight back?

Perhaps we wonder what's the point? Bad guys with money and power almost always get away with their atrocities, even after the war is over. What can any of us do against an industry that's more powerful than the most powerful government on the planet?

Let's try to remember that this fight isn't about justice for fossil fuel Nazis. It's about *us* escaping the gas chambers.

Maybe we're already heroes like the German and Danish officials who tipped off the Jewish community in Denmark the day before they were set to be rounded up, actions that ended up saving 99% of the country's Jewish population, the only occupied nation to save its Jews.

And if we're not, let's *start* being those people.

The question we're all asking ourselves, of course, isn't "Should we?" but "*Can* we?"

In a time of great evil, there's no neutral position. Annie Dillard's observation is useful, whatever our plans: "How we spend our days…is how we spend our lives."

Do we spend our days postponing action? Do we spend *years* postponing action? Our entire lives?

If we don't feel up to the most controversial actions, is there anything else we can do to save ourselves and others from the CO_2 and methane gas chambers?

Some in the resistance created propaganda and leaflets, brought other people into the fight. A few young Dutch women flirted with German soldiers and lured them into the woods for some "alone" time. Those soldiers never came back.

Even some Dutch children playing in the streets ambushed soldiers.

Was there retribution? Yes. Were Nazis killing people anyway?

When we get to examples this serious, we also need to ask if we can push the analogy this far. Are we *really* in that much danger? After all, it's just a few cities burning down each year. Just a few extra strong hurricanes. A few additional crop failures. And even if we really are in danger, just who do we fight? The guilty parties today aren't wearing easily identifiable uniforms.

Maybe it would be better, safer, more proper, to petition the Reichstag, send a sternly worded letter to Hitler himself. Maybe we could come up with some clever chants that would do the trick.

Most of us, I think—me included—are more likely to mimic the Jew in an iconic cartoon who is being lined up against a wall in front of a firing squad along with another man. The second man who's facing execution boldly demands a final cigarette. The first Jew, mortified, whispers nervously, "Don't make trouble."

Can we at least be like the last 300 prisoners in Sobibor who, when they realized they were all ultimately doomed, broke out in a mass revolt and fled into the woods?

Only a few dozen survived. After 250,000 others had been murdered there.

But *none* of them would have lived if they hadn't finally acted together.

There are more than 300 of us who can see what's coming, who understand that more than six million lives are at stake, more than twenty million, more than fifty million. What we face today, of course, is different than what people faced during World War II and may require new tactics. Perhaps drones. Hacking. Running for office. But the one tactic that's *not* effective is letting "someone else" do all the work.

How many Jews, gay men, Roma, and others targeted by the Nazis waited too long before trying to escape or fight back? How many others, like Otto Frank, did the best they could and found it still wasn't enough?

How long will *we* wait before we recognize that the danger we face requires more of us than simply shaking our heads in disgust at the latest headline?

When the stakes include our lives, the lives of our friends and family, the survival of thousands of other species, and of civilization itself, how do *we* define "by any means necessary"?

If the acts required to effectuate change compromise our personal ethics beyond the breaking point, we may have to accept that we just aren't up to the challenge. It's okay to know our limits. We're all going to die someday, even if we reach the century mark first. The ability to look in the mirror in the meantime, to live with ourselves, is as important as life itself. And having those limits can force us to find alternate solutions we *can* live with.

Whatever actions we personally decide are worth trying, let's do *something* before that gas chamber door is locked firmly behind us.

Miep Gies, one of Otto Frank's employees who helped hide him and seven other Jews, hated when people told her what an extraordinary thing she'd done. She felt it was a cop out, that it gave people an excuse for not doing what needed to be done. "My story," she said, "is a story of very ordinary people during extraordinarily terrible times."

What will our story be?

And in what world will others reflect on our actions if we don't write a successful one?

Sleeping behind a bank in Seattle.

Living in RVs in Seattle.

Right-Wing Christians Worship a Snowflake God

Many pundits, psychologists, and humanitarians debate the hold Donald Trump has over such a large portion of the evangelical Christian electorate. Why do these voters choose a nasty, vile authoritarian who seems not to embody a single Christian value?

It's because they're tired of a snowflake God.

The God many right-wing Christians worship is terrified of women thinking for themselves. Their god is repulsed by poor people. He pisses his robe when a trans woman enters a public restroom. This "almighty" God trembles in his sandals when children read books about school integration.

Who *wouldn't* get tired of a god like this? Of *course* right-wing Christians want a leader with more backbone.

Sure, it's still a mystery why they choose such a repellent man as Trump. Why not a Gandhi or Martin Luther King Jr.? Why not a Lumumba or Allende?

Oh, wait. Despite being sick of their god, they've still been raised by him and are cowed by any skin color darker than the snowflake they worship.

So what are the rest of us to do? We can't reason with snowflakes who are panic-stricken by reason.

Many on the far right have labeled themselves the "Lost Cause." We may need to accept that they are. Just as there's no longer hope of halting global warming, all we can do now is mitigate the damage caused by snowflake worshipers.

And we don't mitigate damage by allowing "our" guy to support genocide. We don't mitigate damage by allowing our leaders to deny healthcare and education and public transit and childcare and housing to all citizens who need it.

Why would far-right voters tired of a snowflake god want a snowflake president, afraid to serve the people who put him in office? Of *course* they prefer a strongman who mocks us. What we're doing by pushing a milquetoast on ourselves is beyond mockable.

The opposite of milquetoast isn't asshole—it's someone who stands for something even when there's political and corporate opposition. And "the left" certainly has little of that.

If there are no local leaders worth voting for, let's run for office ourselves. Let's then run for state office. Some of us need to stop being similarly fragile snowflakes and run for national office, too. If we're not in a position to run, let's at least get actively involved in campaigning for those who insist on more than incremental change and mild reform.

Many on the right want nothing more than to follow. What *we* need to do is stop being just as sheeplike and start to lead, at whatever level we're currently capable of. Running for office doesn't even need to always be about "winning." We can use the opportunity to educate voters and to learn more ourselves while we're at it.

We unionize our workplaces. We support other workers. We mentally and financially prepare for a potential general strike in 2028.

We rally, we march, we protest. On the many serious issues we face. On just one if that's all we can manage. We call our senators and representatives. We meet them in their offices.

We don't cross our fingers and keep hoping that somehow, someday, soulless corporations will miraculously become human. We don't roll over and say, "Oh, there's nothing we can do." We don't wait for a strongman, vile or otherwise, to do the work for us.

Climate change is an existential threat, if not to our species, then certainly to our civilization. But until we stop limiting ourselves to snowflakes, milquetoasts, and tyrants, we won't be able to address that problem or any other.

While many on the far right are snowflakes, they've learned that worshiping other snowflakes gets them nowhere. It would be a lesson we'd do well to learn ourselves. Let's stop being terrified of real change. Let's stop wishing for it. "Thoughts and prayers" don't *do* anything.

Let's *make* humanitarian progress happen.

Let's Preserve LGBTQ Culture

We must preserve LGBTQ content while we can.

Russia has laws against "gay propaganda." In Hungary and other eastern European nations there are varying degrees of discrimination and censorship as well.

In the U.S., right-wing lawmakers and school boards are already banning some LGBTQ books. They've announced publicly their goal to label all LGBTQ content as "pornographic" and then use that label to ban all LGBTQ content in America.

If U.S. Republicans win in November, this growing threat—and growing reality—could become national law almost overnight. While the U.S. seems to be most at risk right now, every western nation has far-right enemies who would erase us.

One way we can preserve LGBTQ books, music, film, and other material is to vote for candidates who don't support a fascist theocracy. We must get involved, even run for office ourselves, in local elections and not focus solely on national races.

Of course, as we saw on January 6, 2021, voting for democracy may not be enough. As a friend of mine in Canada told me recently, "If Trump wins in November, all hell will break loose. But if Trump loses, all hell will break loose."

Friends in Portugal and Italy have shared the same concerns. Some European nations don't seem to have any LGBTQ archives at all, which means that even absent deliberate persecution, our histories could disappear.

As a teen, I recorded family history while my oldest relatives were still around to tell their stories. I worked in a public library for four years. I wrote the first book on the Upstairs Lounge fire and was an associate producer on the documentary *Upstairs Inferno*. I believe in documenting and preserving history.

I've studied enough history to know we aren't immune to fascism and dictatorship in the U.S. While I fervently hope we avoid it here, it would be foolish not to prepare. It's not defeatist. It's self-defense.

So...what do we do while also fighting to save democracy?

The same thing I do when I write a novel—I save back-ups.

I've donated my Upstairs Lounge research and other materials to ONE Archives in Los Angeles. Other LGBTQ archives in the U.S. include the Tretter Collection in Minneapolis, the GLBT Historical Society in San Francisco, and the Leather Archives in Chicago. But there are several other LGBTQ archives around the world, and we can send some material to each of them. As a writer, I'm not supposed to use clichés, but "Don't put all your eggs in one basket" sounds fitting here.

There's IHLIA in Amsterdam, QRAB in Gothenburg, the Schwules Museum in Berlin, Forum Queeres in Munich,

The ArQuives in Toronto, the Bishopsgate Institute in London, Collectif Archives LGBTQI in Paris, the Cassero Center in Bologna, and more.

These archives accept personal papers, LGBTQ artwork, DVDs, bumper stickers, T-shirts, photos, wedding announcements, lecture notices, syllabi, info on gay bowling leagues or biking groups or senior potlucks or men's choruses, lesbian music festival notices, and any other material that could help future historians understand LGBTQ culture in our times. We can videotape brief oral histories or donate our journals as well, requesting that sensitive material not be made accessible to researchers until after our death (or even a certain length of time after our death).

We should contact the archives first with details of what we want to donate. Different archives specialize in different materials, and all archives have limited space. What that mostly means is they don't want duplicates. If they already have a specific book or film, they may not want a second copy.

But if we have anything original—handwritten manuscripts, old letters (remember those?), or even printed email correspondence—most of these archives will be happy to accept it. Twenty of my original gay patchwork quilts are in ONE Archives in Los Angeles. Original charcoal nudes given to me decades ago I've since gifted to IHLIA in Amsterdam. QRAB in Gothenburg has the artwork I commissioned from a gay Portuguese artist for the cover of *Orgy at the STD Clinic*, a novel which is itself a document of political turmoil during the pandemic.

Over the past year, I've sent more materials to other LGBTQ archives around the world. There's no guarantee those archives will be safe, either. Fascism and intolerance can rise anywhere. It's important for all of us, wherever we are, however safe we feel, to document our lives.

And we should share the wealth, because we don't want a Library of Alexandria event where our one main LGBTQ archive burns to the ground, with priceless items lost forever.

While mailing materials to other countries is expensive, we should also consider donating funds to help cover any import fees on their end or simply to support their ongoing work. Even if we have no materials of our own to donate, we can still send them a few dollars.

Just as preserving LGBTQ history requires a multi-pronged approach, doing so is only one part of preserving democracy. Let's rally, let's march, let's campaign for strong candidates, let's vote, and let's make sure our nations become safer places for everyone.

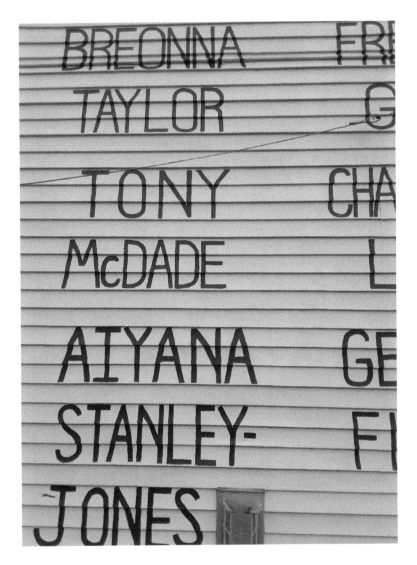

Wall of names, Black Lives Matter.

Lot filled with tiny houses in Seattle.

A General Strike Against Fossil Fuels

What will it take before governments take climate breakdown seriously?

We've tried education and petitions and protests and blocking streets and similar measures for decades and so far have found little success. Whatever "gains" we've made, the fact remains we still pump out more greenhouse gases every year.

How can we *force* change?

Let's coordinate a general strike!

Workers have long known that the only way to force employers to compensate them fairly is to withhold their labor—go on strike.

Strikes are the way we won an 8-hour workday, a 40-hour work week. It's the way we won vacation and sick leave. We won safety measures and anti-discrimination policies. Some workers have won parental leave, family medical leave, and more.

Employers don't part with money or power voluntarily, even if they accumulated that money and power from the labor of others. But standing together in solidarity, workers can claim what's theirs.

We all have the primal human right to a survivable climate, but we can't enjoy even that basic right without demanding it.

Governments won't act out of the goodness of their hearts.

They won't act because it's the right thing to do, not even to save their own children and grandchildren.

They won't act unless we force them.

Let's force them.

It's notoriously difficult to gain enough consensus even within a single company to authorize a strike, much less coordinate that consensus among multiple companies and municipal governments.

But it *has* been done.

The 1919 general strike in Seattle and the 1946 general strike in Oakland didn't accomplish everything workers needed, and those were both localized to small regions, not entire states or countries.

But even a partial general strike can achieve results.

The 1975 Women's Strike in Iceland pushed the country's parliament to guarantee equal pay.

Perhaps we can concentrate on one industry in multiple states or countries. Or multiple industries in a single city or state that is heavily reliant on fossil fuel corporations. A general strike doesn't need to include the entire planet.

Yet.

But we need some real victories, and the methods we're currently using aren't getting the job done.

To be effective, a general climate strike can't be merely a one-day demonstration. Corporations and governments can bear that easily enough. We must strike until we see meaningful legislation.

The obvious obstacle to success is that those in power *do* have power. They'll make it illegal to "disrupt" the economy. They'll ban "sympathy" strikes, try to break unions. They'll even order police or hired thugs to physically attack us.

There are real consequences to fighting fossil fuel corporations and the politicians they buy.

But there are real consequences for not doing so, too.

In many parts of the U.S., we can no longer purchase homeowners or flood insurance. State economies suffer billion-dollar disasters year after year, and those disasters keep growing more expensive.

We *will* experience increasing drought and crop failures. We *will* witness more wildfires wiping out entire towns. We *will* suffer stronger storms and heavier flooding.

These won't just be disturbing news stories or temporary inconveniences. We can already see societal breakdown. That will also escalate as suffering people—even those who don't understand who is causing their suffering—become radicalized.

Internal documents from fossil fuel corporations prove that researchers were aware decades ago that climate change could threaten civilization.

The planet won't die. Even during the worst mass extinction events, some life goes on. It's likely even some humans will survive the end of civilization.

But you probably won't. I won't. Our loved ones probably won't.

A general strike is risky.

But when someone breaks into your home and starts attacking you and your family, you take whatever risks you must to save yourself and those you love.

None of us want to be in this situation. Yet it's been forced upon us. We've asked politely for change. We've asked impolitely.

Not it's time to force the issue.

Workers have power if we use it. Strikes succeed if we don't give in. So let's contact the leaders of our unions and climate organizations and start coordinating a general strike against fossil fuels while we still have a chance to make a difference.

The Great Replacement Theory Infiltrates the LGBTQ Community

Growing up white in the Deep South, I of course received my share of Replacement Theory indoctrination. "You see those little pillows on the back dash of that car?" My mom pointed to a maroon car with two identical maroon pillows in the corners of the rear window. "That's a secret code black people have." She didn't say "black people," of course. "It means they all want to have at least five babies so they can outnumber us and take over the country."

This was back in the early 1970s, and of course The Great Replacement Theory, in one form or another, has been around for much longer than that.

I never expected it to take its latest form, though. A friend of mine who immigrated to Europe with his husband to escape the growing fascism in the U.S. has learned that there's a new plot to destroy the gay community.

"Religious conservatives are forcing their gay and lesbian kids to transition," he told me. "They aren't as embarrassed with a trans daughter as they are with a gay son or vice versa. They figure their kids will pass better if they transition early. Ten thousand minors have been forced to transition so far. They're going to erase gays and lesbians from society!"

I admit I was floored. "Um, what conservative religion is doing *that*?" I asked. I grew up Mormon, with Southern Baptist relatives. I attended a Baptist high school, did two years as a Mormon missionary in Italy. I'd never heard of such an attitude before.

"It's all this woke nonsense," he went on. "Progressives are supporting it because they're afraid to say anything that might be interpreted as transphobic. So we're participating in our own destruction!"

"All I see on the news," I said, "is religious conservatives ranting about the evils of trans people."

"Oh, but you only see what Mainstream Media wants you to see," he said. "Here in Europe, we get more news. You can't help your ignorance. That's why I'm telling you what I've learned."

"I do watch news from Germany, France, Italy, and the UK," I said.

"But you watch it in America. You don't see what's really happening."

He said "lots" was happening in the UK and then also mentioned Iran, but I couldn't quite believe a government that executed gay men would push trans surgery on anyone. And ten thousand children? Really?

Just on the face of it, the claims seemed ridiculous.

My friend sent me links, but I didn't open them. I already follow several informative trans YouTube channels (Jessie

Gender and Jammidodger, for starters) who offer great, authoritative information. I suspected my friend was hearing misinformation, and I didn't want to open a link that was malicious, with or without malware attached.

"You're burying your head in the sand!" my friend said. "You're as bad as MAGA."

I told my friend I didn't want to discuss the subject with him any longer. Over the following weeks, I browsed videos from several additional trans people I considered authorities and never saw the accusation raised at all. There was some talk about minors receiving little or no counseling, doctors moving directly to medical treatment. That did sound problematic. And a few detransitioning adults said they'd decided on their own it would be easier to escape the judgment of their religion by choosing a different gender.

But there was no mention of religious leaders or parents pushing transitioning as a solution to the sin of homosexuality, and nothing about huge numbers in this or *any* category of regretful minors or adults. My friend and I talked weekly, and over the next month, he kept bringing up the danger of gay erasure through forced transitioning again and again.

"I've asked you not to discuss this with me," I said. "Please respect my boundaries."

"Okay, I won't talk about it again. But we'll have to talk about it sooner or later because all this woke poison is destroying the gay community by forcing kids to transition."

My friend and I are currently taking a break from our weekly calls.

The Great Replacement Theory, in whatever form it takes, replaces reason with delusion. It replaces friendship with alienation, solidarity with division.

But it's an effective strategy. It works. My friend is both intelligent and highly educated. Yet he got caught up in the madness.

Whether or not minors should receive hormone treatment in addition to counseling may well be debatable, but when your reason for pausing therapy is to prevent gay erasure, you're not approaching trans care from a scientific perspective or even a political one. You're doing it irrationally, and there can be no useful discussion under those conditions.

Sometimes, I feel like we're living through a version of *Invasion of the Body Snatchers*, with pod people taking over the bodies of our loved ones. Perhaps if we shake them back awake before it's too late, we can reclaim them. Often, though, by the time we realize there's a problem, it's already too late.

In *An Underground Life: Memoirs of a Gay Jew in Nazi Berlin*, Gad Beck recounts his years in Berlin during the Holocaust as friends, family, and lovers were killed and deported, never to be seen again. Despite the horrors he witnessed, he always remained positive. Near the end of his account, he talks of the importance of surrounding oneself with others who have positive attitudes, saying something along the lines of, "If someone is always unhappy and focusing on the negative, there's nothing you can do to change that. It's their nature." He said he learned to avoid their company.

His assessment sounded harsh, and I don't think it's always true. Besides, they were in the middle of the Holocaust! Of *course* other Jews and gay men were unhappy!

But the instinctive need to protect oneself isn't something to dismiss. We can try to talk to friends and families who aren't too far gone, but there comes a point when continuing to do so is not only pointless but also puts our own sanity and safety in jeopardy.

I can reach out to my friend again in a couple of months and see if there's been any change, reassessing the situation at that time. In all likelihood, he'll have dug his heels in even further.

But maybe not. We'll see.

What's important for all of us in these situations is to accept that truth and friendship don't always win. We must find a way to accept loss and mourn appropriately without losing ourselves in the process.

Perhaps one day, someone living through the collapse of American democracy and the fall of capitalism will write a memoir of their own, leaving behind advice for the next generation. Let's try to make the best decisions we can so we'll actually have some worthwhile advice to share.

And so we can remain sane and safe during these troubled times.

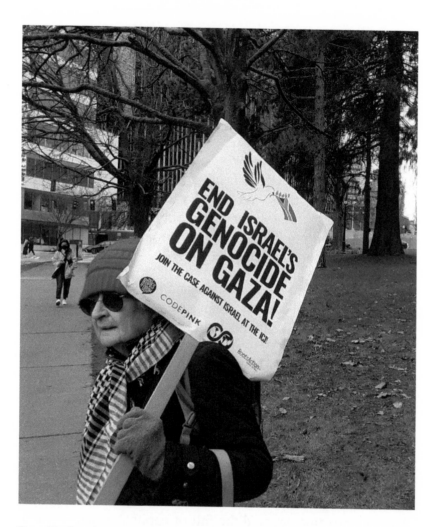

Pro-Palestine protest in Seattle

Austerity Is Not Responsible Governance

The *Seattle Times* editorial board warns against the "ballooning salaries of public employees." A 1% Cost-of-Living-Adjustment in the face of 16% inflation is not, of course, a raise. It's a 15% pay cut. Even a 16% COLA would only be maintaining the status quo.

The editorial board complains that 6320 of 14006 City employees have a base rate of over $100K a year. But they ignore the 7686 public employees who *don't* earn that impressive salary.

The contract bargaining taking place now addresses those lesser paid employees. **And over 65% of the employees whose wages are being cut are *not* paid from the General Fund.**

Still, that figure of 6320 public workers making $100K looks damning. The implication is that a lifeguard is raking in tons of cash while just lying in a swimsuit beside the pool, that a cashier at the zoo is browsing online between customers to decide which yacht to buy.

The implication is that a horde of lazy, unproductive people are leeches on society.

Cashiers and customer service reps and lifeguards and library workers aren't making $100,000 a year.

The mayor is. So are City attorneys. Lots of high-ranking folks are, both in and out of the public sector.

But we're talking about 6320 jobs. That's more than just a few people at the top. So just who *are* these folks?

Well, every Seattle police officer employed by the City for at least three and a half years earns more than $100K. So does every Seattle firefighter on staff at least three and a half years.

There are almost 1000 Seattle police officers, almost 1000 Seattle firefighters.

Is the editorial board of the *Seattle Times* proposing to cut pay for police officers and firefighters? Or only keep these workers for three years and then cast them aside once they start earning too much, forcing a turnover to ensure we're always staffed with the least experienced workers?

There's a reason those demanding austerity don't specify who the lowest paid workers are. Implications against a fair contract only succeed without facts.

Labor advocates fighting for a fair contract aren't begrudging police officers, firefighters, and City attorneys their income. We're saying the rest of us have bills to pay, too. We need to provide food for our families like everyone else, pay our rent, hopefully one day own a home.

If our jobs serve the public and fill a need, then they're essential for a functioning society and need to be compensated with a living wage.

Until society can be run by bots, we need humans to fill those jobs, and humans have bills to pay.

The Tacoma Housing Authority just raised its minimum wage to $32 an hour because it discovered that too many of its own employees needed housing assistance. Rents and mortgages are even more expensive in Seattle.

To address chronic understaffing and attrition, San Juan County in Washington state recently agreed to a 32-hour/four-day work week at 40 hours pay. Nationally, striking United Auto Workers are raising that same demand.

At a recent meeting with city council members and candidates, one City worker shared that he had resorted to selling blood plasma to make ends meet. A building inspector revealed that many on his team lived outside Seattle and yet were essential in responding to disasters like earthquakes and landslides. He pointed out what should be obvious—it would be useful if those workers were able to live reasonably close to where they'll be needed during an emergency.

A recent article in the *Seattle Times*, one the editorial board of that paper surely read, revealed that to purchase a starter home in Seattle, a homeowner would need to earn at least $142K a year. That leaves out even those 6320 "overpaid" workers the editorial board complains about.

Seattle City Light just announced they were raising their rates by 10%, meaning the City's COLA offer won't even keep pace with their own contribution to inflation.

At a Labor Day rally the day after the pro-austerity editorial was published, City of Seattle council member and labor advocate Teresa Mosqueda pointed out that public workers are carrying a heavier workload than ever before.

The latest census shows that Seattle's population increased by over 128,000 in the past decade.

More residents in the city means we need more housing. It means we have more Seattle City Light customers, more residents who need garbage pickup and water service. It means more residents who need access to libraries and parks.

Food insecurity has increased dramatically in the past few years. The percentage of low-income households in Seattle that need monthly food assistance is 26% in some neighborhoods, up to 55% in others.

The latest statistics show that homelessness has increased by 10% in the last couple of years in Seattle and King County, a problem requiring services at multiple levels. There's an increasing need for public sector workers to address the chaos created by the mayor and pro-corporate city council members who refuse to establish rent control or tax Seattle's tax-dodging corporations.

Instead of governing responsibly, Mayor Harrell told the bargaining team to "Rally your asses off!"

And yet when the Coalition moved ahead with the rally, the Mayor's office then sent the unions a "Cease and Desist" letter threatening to take legal action if union workers rallied. The letter was filled with inaccurate claims and was a clear intimidation tactic—which failed. Fifteen hundred workers and supporters showed up to rally at City Hall. Some wore shirts that read "Rally your asses off!"

The Coalition of City Unions is organizing practice picketing on November 2 at Seattle Municipal Tower, Seattle Center, and other worksites to show the mayor and city council they are making demands, not requests. If you're local, show your support by joining the practice picket lines. Ask your friends and neighbors to turn out. City workers already have the support of the community they serve. Now Mayor Harrell and the city council need to **see** that support.

We need a fair contract to keep the workers we have and attract additional workers to make up for the 14% vacancy rate in many departments. We also need to increase the number of positions in those departments to serve the increased number of residents and increased needs of those residents.

The editorial board of the *Seattle Times* may champion austerity all it wants, but demanding a pay cut for the workers who keep Seattle running is more than just callously out of touch. Such a policy is also bad for business. It's bad for residents. And it's simply bad governance.

Rally at Seattle City Hall on September 19, 2023

Resources

Crosscut: "Seattle city employees say low pay, safety contribute to vacancies," Josh Cohen, Aug. 21, 2023

King 5: "City of Seattle employees rally as union negotiations continue," Sept. 20, 2023

KNKX NPR: "In midst of budget deliberations, Seattle workers push for more pay," Lily Ana Fowler, Sept. 28, 2023

KUOW NPR: "Mayor Harrell wades into labor dispute with city workers amid budget dilemma," Monica Nickelsburg, Aug. 17, 2023

Publicola: "Months into contract negotiations, City unions say Harrell Has Barely Budged on Pay," Erica C. Barnett, Aug. 17, 2023

Real Change: "City workers rally for a better labor contract," Guy Oron, Sept. 27, 2023

Seattle Times: "Seattle workers rally for new contract, express outrage over city proposal," Daisy Zavala Magaña, Sept. 19, 2023

Seattle Times: "You're not imagining it—costs in Seattle rose faster than San Francisco," Alison Saldanha, June 20, 2023

The Stand: "More than 1000 Seattle city workers rally for #RSPCT," Coalition of City Unions, Sept. 20, 2023

The Stranger: "City workers rally their asses off," Hannah Krieg, Sept. 20, 2023

July 4th rally at Lenin statue in Seattle.

How to Make Public Comments at City Budget Hearings

In Seattle, the city council has budget hearings in October and November. The public has two opportunities to make public comments, either in person in the council chambers or remotely by phone during the hearing. Folks can sign up two hours before the start of each session. Your city or county likely does something similar, and you can find details on the corresponding website.

It can feel intimidating to speak publicly, and it almost always feels pointless. Politicians will do what they want, won't they, regardless of what "the people" want?

But I've attended both public hearings this year, and I do think **speaking up makes a difference, especially when council members—and other city residents—hear the same issues raised again and again.**

In Seattle, the problems that residents raise most often include the need for more "tiny houses" for the unhoused, ending sweeps, and more funding for services to address our worsening homelessness crisis. Some speakers keep a tally of unhoused people who have died on the streets (it's 300 so far this year). Others demand solutions for the shockingly high number of pedestrians killed by vehicles in the city (over 30 so far).

Students beg for funding to increase the number of mental healthcare professionals in schools. Gig workers demand passing a fee to fund enforcement of regulations to protect them from employer abuses. People debate the effectiveness of ShotSpotter.

With all the problems a city faces, you'll find that only a handful of topics come up again and again. That's what makes speaking on them important.

Here are some simple tips to make the process less nerve racking for those of us prone to nervousness:

Write your comments down ahead of time. Have two versions, one that lasts ninety seconds and another that lasts two minutes. Depending on how many people sign up to speak, you'll have one of those two windows to make your point. The first public hearing I attended lasted over three hours, the second over four hours. In that last hearing, 60 people made their public comments in person while another 96 gave them over the phone.

When I printed out my statement, I used the color shading feature on Word to highlight every other sentence in bright yellow, to help me keep my place as I read, in case my nervousness distracted me.

Practice! Read out both versions of your public comment several times. Out loud. It's the only way you won't stumble when the time comes. And it's the only way to know for sure your comments fit the time slot.

State your name for the record. You can include what district you live or work in, but remember that your time is limited. Get to your message quickly.

Be prepared to **address a specific point** on the agenda. A link to the agenda will be provided on the city's website. You'll probably need to reference it simply to be able to fill out the sign-up form.

Don't insult the city council members, no matter how tempted you are. The hearing is to address specific items about the budget, not the moral character of the council members. Offending the people you need to support your agenda item isn't an effective way to get them to support that item.

If you're attending the hearing in person, wear a shirt that carries a message. Depending on your city's guidelines, you may be permitted to bring in a small sign. Often, the sign can't have a stick to support it, the sticks considered potential weapons.

If you speak in person, watch those who go before you and see how close to get to the microphone. Some people are too far away and can barely be heard. Others are so close their voices are muffled. Watch and hear what works best.

There will likely be additional guidelines for those who attend in person. Clapping, cheering, or booing the comments of others slows things down, and the meeting will already be long. You'll probably be encouraged to wave your hands to show non-auditory support for the comments others make.

If you speak by phone, be aware that there will be instructions on how to unmute your phone. It won't be a matter of hitting the Unmute button. Perhaps you'll have to hit *6 or some other simple combination of characters.

Speak clearly and slowly. If you have so much to say that you need to rush to fit it all in, cut something out. You can't say everything that needs to be said. But make sure what you *do* say can be heard by the council members *and* by the other residents attending. I learned about issues I wasn't even aware of while listening to others speak.

If you have a friend or coworker or family member who will participate with you, divide your message to cover more ground. Have one person give statistics and anecdotes while another attacks the topic from another angle. In general, stories are a powerful tool.

Start with your request and conclude with a call to action.

We only need to attend one or two hearings a year. It's okay to feel a bit bored or tired. But it's still a short time investment for something that will impact us every other day of the year. If we're involved in a long-term battle, we may find ourselves saying the same things again and again, but that's okay, too. There's a reason advertisers use the same words when promoting a brand or product—repetition eventually communicates a message.

Here's the two-minute version of my public comment, which I submitted in writing to the city council the day after the public hearing, during which I'd only been able to give a ninety-second version of the statement:

> I urge you to increase the Amazon tax and ensure a fair contract for City workers.

> Equity isn't free.

A functioning infrastructure isn't free.

Living wages don't materialize out of nowhere.

It would be great to live in a world that ran smoothly—no poverty, no crime, no potholes, everything clean, everything wonderful—without having to pay for it.

But living in a great city doesn't happen on its own just because we're all good people.

It costs money to make a city livable.

And that money can only come from those who have it.

You can't tax homeless people and folks living in poverty and expect to fund a decent infrastructure.

Even the middle class alone don't have enough to pay for it.

The money *has* to come from the wealthy and from corporations, too.

The rest of us are already paying our fair share…and we're happy to keep doing so. We understand that a society cannot function without adequate taxation.

But those with the least money simply don't have enough to do it by ourselves.

City workers need a living wage.

City residents need libraries and parks and police and firefighters and trash collectors and safe streets.

And that means the wealthy and corporations must pay their fair share just like the rest of us already do.

Of course, you can let the wealthy pressure you into exempting them.

But if you don't get the money the city needs from those who have it, you end up with workers leaving because they can't afford to live here.

City services suffer.

Residents suffer.

Tourists have a bad experience and tell their friends.

We end up with unhoused folks just being swept from place to place, the problem only growing worse.

There are only two options—provide infrastructure or don't provide infrastructure.

If we choose to provide it, there's only one source of revenue—tax the people who have the money. It's not rocket science.

We live in one of the richest cities in the country, in one of the richest countries in the world, one of the richest cities in the history of civilization.

If we can't fund living wages for City workers and a functioning infrastructure for Seattle residents, with all the money we have here, it's a gross failure of leadership.

We ask that you choose not to fail but to succeed.

Remember, we don't have to be eloquent. We only need to make our voices heard. And we can only be heard if we speak out.

Let's speak out.

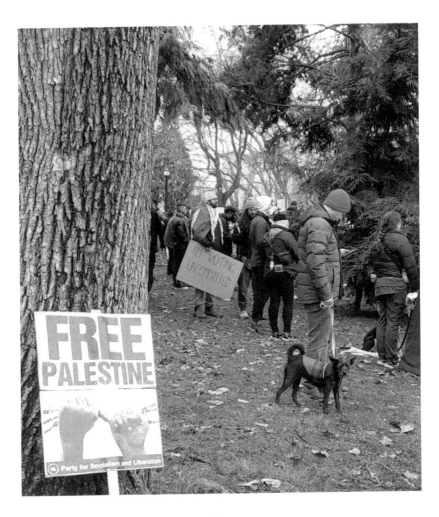

Pro-Palestine rally in Seattle.

Rationing Water in the Midst of Record Rainfall

People are dying of thirst in Seattle. We've had record rainfall the past few years. We have snow melt feeding into the Duwamish River that provides fresh water. We have 8.2 quintillion gallons of fresh water in Lake Union. Another 2.9 cubic kilometers of fresh water (many times more than in Lake Union) in Lake Washington. There's nearby Lake Sammamish, too. We're only a few miles from a temperate rain forest.

But Seattle officials have chosen to hoard all this water and ration only a few quarts here and there. 750,000 people are suffering. Some are dying.

Put another way, Seattle's mayor and city council have decided to only push property tax levies to fund essential city services, squeezing water from a stone. In one of the richest cities in the country, in one of the richest countries in the world, in one of the richest cities in the history of civilization, Seattle's "leaders" have chosen not to use the wealth all around them to serve the city's residents.

The Seattle Public Library, facing both a funding and staffing shortage, is implementing rolling closures at every branch one day a week. Back in December, a coalition of unions finally won a tentative agreement for city workers after two years without a contract. Despite inflation of more than 18% since workers received their last Cost-of-Living-Adjustment, the new contract offered only a 5% COLA for 2023 and a 4.5% COLA for 2024.

And despite union members approving the contract, the city council didn't make their final vote until April. The COLA adjustments still won't go into effect until the end of May. And retroactive pay for 2023 and the first five months of 2024 won't be issued until October, without interest.

With inflation for the first quarter of 2024 already at 3.5%, it looks as if this year's COLA will continue to amount to another pay cut. The COLA for the following two years is capped at similar levels to ensure additional pay cuts if inflation continues as it has the past four.

City leaders have also instituted a hiring freeze. There are continuing staff shortages in virtually every department and at almost every level. This leaves us with trash everywhere, people living in cars and RVs and tents and sleeping bags. There are long wait times to receive permits, to talk to customer service agents in public utilities, to address water leaks. There are longer wait times for *everything*.

The mayor has announced his "One Seattle" plan to "revitalize" downtown and bring everyone together. But there's a reason his plan isn't working.

The mayor and city council are essentially keeping all the water for the wealthiest residents, who then sell it at $100 a gallon to their friends, at $500 a gallon to almost everyone else, while refusing to sell it at any price to those they like least.

The people who the mayor and city council refuse to serve call this plan "1% Seattle." The wealthy are served quite well, as always, but the rest of us are suffering dehydration and kidney failure.

Mind you, this is a problem at the county and state level as well. There's not even a state income tax here.

Do you know what you can buy with $0?

Nothing.

Public health and other public services are funded largely through regressive taxation—sales tax and property tax. But despite Seattle's high rates, regressive taxes can never be enough to fund essential services.

Those who don't care about libraries or public health or parks or public utilities might want to note that these shortages also impact the fire and police departments, both also significantly understaffed.

When you ration or outright deny water to residents in the midst of record rainfall, you're not only inflicting untold misery on others but also creating a dystopia you must constantly navigate yourself.

Those at the top are addicted to their power and wealth. They're unable to stop abusing their drug of choice. Pointing out the obvious isn't a solution, of course.

So what *is* the solution?

It's up to us to force these addicts into rehab so they finally face their addictions and stop abusing the rest of us, too.

But "rehab" can't be created with incremental reform that these addicts are in a position to overturn. What we need is socialism. That's become painfully obvious, too.

As obvious as an empty glass without even a drop of water left to drink, in a world that's hotter every day.

Work with the Volunteer You Have, Not the Volunteer You Wish You Had

A friend of mine, let's call him Jared, was asked to lead a class on the history of Palestine. He'd been participating in protests against the genocide in Gaza almost weekly for several months. Years before, he'd taken a course on Middle Eastern history as an elective. He agreed to lead the discussion and read all the material for the first lesson, preparing for many hours. He bought snacks with his own funds for the ten people who showed up in person. Another eight participated via Zoom.

He'd hardly made it back to his apartment before the person who'd asked him to accept this assignment called and began critiquing his performance. Jared hadn't done this right. He hadn't done that right. He'd missed an opportunity there. He wasn't taking this seriously.

This director, let's call her Cindy, had behaved similarly many times before. In our weekly phone calls, Jared complained dozens of times about Cindy's harsh critiques. This time, Jared had had enough. "I told her this was the last assignment I'd accept."

In our zeal to make the world a better place, let's not make ourselves miserable by demanding too much of ourselves. Just as importantly, let's not make others miserable, either.

I'm not nearly the volunteer my friend Jared is. In fact, I do less than most of my friends. I used to feel guilty, chastising myself. "I should do more."

Yes, I should. But I've learned to accept my limitations. I accept that others are better volunteers, better advocates, better activists. It's *okay* not to be the best. Even the most impressive activists, after all, rarely *solve* a problem. Greta Thunberg is genuinely awe-inspiring and has moved the needle, but global warming still worsens. Aaron Bushnell self-immolated to protest the genocide in Gaza, but as of this writing, that genocide continues.

None of us should discourage others from doing their utmost to help confront these or other problems. Let's be supportive in every way we can of their efforts. We can do that while still recognizing *our* limits and making our personal boundaries clear to those who keep asking more and more of us.

"You're being selfish." "You're being weak." Whatever the accusation, it's an ad hominem attack. We won't get far without assuming good intent from the people on our side.

Guilt is a poor motivator, and when it's coupled with criticism for our inevitably less than stellar performance, it crushes our spirits. People with crushed spirits rarely start performing *better*.

Morally, these harsh critiques are wrong. Strategically, they're ineffective.

Constructive criticism of Jared's lesson might have been okay—but only after Cindy thanked him for his time, effort, preparation, and snack donation. Not to mention his loyal commitment to the organization. But when my friend Jared recounts the things Cindy tells him, they sound more like judgment and condemnation. Berating folks who are doing their best—or even less than their best but still *volunteering*—leads to fewer folks volunteering.

At my mother's wake, I hung out with several of her friends. I'd long had older friends and knew a couple of these folks apart from their relationship with my mom. They were my friends, too. At one point, someone told a funny story, and everyone laughed, including me. They then looked horrified. How could I possibly laugh at my mother's wake? They may have felt guilty themselves, realizing they were laughing, too. The group quickly broke up and went their separate ways, leaving me alone.

Being "abandoned" at such a difficult time was hardly the support I needed. I remember thinking, "Hey, guys, I can be sad any time. What's hard is being happy. I was happy for a moment, and then you left."

The same is true when we work in climate organizations, working to find housing for the unhoused, when confronting fascism.

We don't *need* to be miserable out of solidarity. It's okay to have fun, to smile, laugh, even if others are suffering. There will always be others suffering and we'll have more strength to help if we're not depleted by our own misery. We fear our joy, however brief, is an insult to the miserable, but our misery doesn't help them, either.

We don't need to make ourselves miserable to be "good," but just as importantly, we don't need to make others miserable, either. Volunteering, advocacy, and activism are marathons, not sprints. We won't make the distance if we're already in severe pain by mile two.

As a Mormon missionary in Italy, I was required to participate in daily "Devotionals" and weekly "District Meetings." At these meetings, we were required to declare our goals for the day or week and then go over our goals from the previous meeting and compare how we'd performed with what our expectations had been. Since exceedingly few Catholics in Rome were interested in converting to Mormonism, most missionaries consistently "failed" to deliver on their goals. The result was public reprimands, public humiliation, public calls to step up and do better.

Of course, we rarely did better, regardless of our efforts. What our leaders succeeded in accomplishing, though, was making our lives miserable. My first bout of clinical depression developed when I *volunteered* as a missionary. I was paying my own way, postponing college for two years, and being told every day I didn't measure up.

Non-Mormons hear this and think, "Why did you put up with that crap?"

And yet many of us in climate organizations, political organizations, or whatever other volunteer group we're affiliated with, put up with similar treatment.

We're trying to make the world a better place, dealing with horror, misery, and oppression in our personal lives, in our communities, and across the globe. The last thing we need is to be made miserable when trying to offer what we can to help others.

As a Mormon, I was taught that when the bishop over our congregation asked us to accept a "calling," it was as if God himself was asking. Technically, we could say no, but who could say no to God? We were essentially guilted into accepting every work assignment thrust upon us.

I taught Sunday School, I taught the deacons, I prepared and passed the sacrament, I sold Church magazine subscriptions, I visited four families in the congregation every month, I collected fast offerings, I organized Single Adult dances and canoe trips, I taught the Elders Quorum. I can't even remember all the "callings" I accepted.

But I do remember the one time I said no. I'd been guilted into becoming the ward membership clerk. This meant I needed to keep track of every Mormon living within ward boundaries. Who lived where, who'd moved away, who'd moved in. This included members who hadn't set foot inside a church in years. Bishops in other states who tracked members leaving their congregations would send us notice of folks moving into our area.

This included folks who didn't want to be tracked at all, but that's another story.

When I accepted the assignment, the bishop informed me that the previous ward membership clerk had fallen behind. The membership rolls were four months out of date. I struggled with the assignment for three months, miserable the entire time. Finally, I told my bishop I was resigning from the position.

"The rolls are now six months out of date. I just can't do this."

"But we have no one else."

"I'm not doing it anymore."

I learned in my early twenties how to say no, and I must say, it's one of the few important lessons I learned at church. It's not one typically taught by Mormons. But I learned it anyway.

What I've learned since is that it's *okay* to say no. We don't need to explain or justify or come up with an excuse. "No" is a complete sentence.

It's fine to stretch ourselves, try new things, go beyond our comfort zone. And it's okay not to.

"Johnny, we need someone to cook for this upcoming meeting."

"Hmm, I can't do that, but I can help clean up afterward."

It's also okay to negotiate what we will and won't do.

I volunteered to proof articles for a literary journal. Another volunteer refused to proof the endnotes, but that was something I could do. It's not always about saying no. We can sometimes do what others can't.

What crushes us is agreeing to do things we loathe.

My friend Jared is often asked at the last minute to take over an assignment someone else reneged on. The original volunteer had two weeks to prepare. Jared often gets two days. When he inevitably ends up not performing as well as the director wishes, he's harshly critiqued.

"Cindy can't get anyone else to do it," Jared told me, "because they're afraid."

Some organizations thrive and others dwindle away over time. It matters how we treat our volunteers.

Actually, it matters how we treat paid workers, too. But that's another story.

At church, I sang in the ward choir. It wasn't a "calling." I simply enjoyed singing and joined of my own volition. But the choir director was rude. After a couple of months, I quit. This was supposed to be fun.

Sometimes, we need to say no even when the task is something we're good at, something we enjoy. When I volunteered with Jewish Family Services, my assignment was to play pool once a week with a man in his nineties. Who could ask for a better "chore"? But I was on public transit, and it required two buses plus a long walk to reach this man's house. I quickly realized I wasn't up to dedicating four hours a week even for something I enjoyed. I told the volunteer coordinator I would only be able to visit once a month.

Of course she accepted my terms.

It shouldn't feel easier to quit altogether than to say, "I can't do this, but I can do that. Does that work for you? If it doesn't, I'll understand if you need to find someone else."

If we make ourselves miserable, we'll burn out. If we make others miserable, they'll burn out.

Burned out cinders aren't going to make the world a better place.

The next time a volunteer coordinator takes us to task for not doing a better job, let's remember that we can tell them the truth: You need to work with the volunteer you have, not the one you wish you had.

In a perfect world, we'd all be perfect. But the world isn't perfect and neither are we. Let's stop beating ourselves up over it. And let's stop beating our allies up over it, too.

Books by Johnny Townsend

Thanks for reading! If you enjoyed this book, could you please take a few minutes to write a review online? Reviews are helpful both to me as an author and to other readers, so we'd all sincerely appreciate your writing one! And if you did enjoy the book, here are some others I've written you might want to look up:

Mormon Underwear

A Gay Mormon Missionary in Pompeii

The Golem of Rabbi Loew

Marginal Mormons

Sexual Solidarity

The Mysterious Madness of Mormons

Going-Out-Of-Religion Sale

Escape from Zion

Gayrabian Nights

Invasion of the Spirit Snatchers

Sins of the Saints

Mormon Misfits

Gay Gaslighting

Out of the Missionary's Closet

A Mormon Motive for Murder

Breaking the Promise of the Promised Land

Mormon Misfits

I Will, Through the Veil

Am I My Planet's Keeper?

Have Your Cum and Eat It, Too

Strangers with Benefits

Constructing Equity

Wake Up and Smell the Missionaries

Racism by Proxy

Orgy at the STD Clinic

Please Evacuate

Recommended Daily Humanity

The Camper Killings

Repent! The End of Capitalism is Nigh!

Kinky Quilts: Patchwork Designs for Gay Men

An Eternity of Mirrors: Best Short Stories of Johnny Townsend

Inferno in the French Quarter: The UpStairs Lounge Fire

Latter-Gay Saints: An Anthology of Gay Mormon Fiction (co-editor)

Available from your favorite online or neighborhood bookstore.

Wondering what some of those other books are about? Read on!

Invasion of the Spirit Snatchers

During the Apocalypse, a group of Mormon survivors in Hurricane, Utah gather in the home of the Relief Society president, telling stories to pass the time as they ration their food storage and await the Second Coming. But this is no ordinary group of Mormons— or perhaps it is. They are the faithful, feminist, gay, apostate, and repentant, all working together to help each other through the darkest days any of them have yet seen.

Gayrabian Nights

Gayrabian Nights is a twist on the well-known classic, *1001 Arabian Nights*, in which Scheherazade, under the threat of death if she ceases to captivate King Shahryar's attention, enchants him through a series of mysterious, adventurous, and romantic tales.

In this variation, a male escort, invited to the hotel room of a closeted, homophobic Mormon senator, learns that the man is poised to vote on a piece of anti-gay legislation the following morning. To prevent him from sleeping, so that the exhausted senator will miss casting his vote on the Senate floor, the escort entertains him with stories of homophobia, celibacy, mixed orientation marriages, reparative therapy, coming out, first love, gay marriage, and long-term successful gay relationships.

The escort crafts the stories to give the senator a crash course in gay culture and sensibilities, hoping to bring the man closer to accepting his own sexual orientation.

Inferno in the French Quarter: The UpStairs Lounge Fire

On Gay Pride Day in 1973, someone set the entrance to a French Quarter gay bar on fire. In the terrible inferno that followed, thirty-two people lost their lives, including a third of the local congregation of the Metropolitan Community Church, their pastor burning to death halfway out a second-story window as he tried to claw his way to freedom.

A mother who'd gone to the bar with her two gay sons died alongside them. A man who'd helped his friend escape first was found dead near the fire escape. Two children waited outside a movie theater across town for a father and "uncle" who would never pick them up. During this era of rampant homophobia, several families refused to claim the bodies, and many churches refused to bury the dead.

Author Johnny Townsend pored through old records and tracked down survivors of the fire as well as relatives and friends of those killed to compile this fascinating account of a forgotten moment in gay history.

This second edition on the 50th anniversary of the fire includes additional research, photos, and information not available previously.

A Gay Mormon Missionary in Pompeii

What is a gay Mormon missionary doing in Italy? He is trying to save his own soul as well as the souls of others. In these tales chronicling the two-year mission of Robert Anderson, we see a young man tormented by his inability to be the man the Church says he should be. In addition to his personal hell, Anderson faces a major earthquake, organized crime, a serious bus accident, and much more. He copes with horrendous mission leaders and his own suicidal tendencies. But one day, he meets another missionary who loves him, and his world changes forever.

The Golem of Rabbi Loew

Jacob and Esau Cohen are the closest of brothers. In fact, they're lovers. A doctor tries to combine canine genes with those of Jews, to improve their chances of surviving a hostile world. A Talmudic scholar dates an escort. A scientist tries to develop the "God spot" in the brains of his patients in hopes of creating a messiah.

A Jew-by-Choice navigates Jewish/Muslim relations during Pesach. A gay Lubavitcher dating a Catholic is attacked and left for dead but becomes a police officer in response. The Golem of Prague is really Rabbi Loew's secret lover.

While some of the Jews in Townsend's book are Orthodox, this collection of Jewish stories most certainly is not.

Am I My Planet's Keeper?

Global Warming. Climate Change. Climate Crisis. Climate Emergency. Whatever label we use, we are facing one of the greatest challenges to the survival of life as we know it.

But while addressing greenhouse gases is perhaps our most urgent need, it's not our only task. We must also address toxic waste, pollution, habitat destruction, and our other contributions to the world's sixth mass extinction event.

In order to do that, we must simultaneously address the unmet human needs that keep us distracted from deeper engagement in stabilizing our climate: moderating economic inequality, guaranteeing healthcare to all, and ensuring education for everyone.

And to accomplish *that*, we must unite to combat the monied forces that use fear, prejudice, and misinformation to manipulate us.

It's a daunting task. But success is our only option.

Wake Up and Smell the Missionaries

Two Mormon missionaries in Italy discover they share the same rare ability—both can emit pheromones on demand. At first, they playfully compete in the hills of Frascati to see who can tempt "investigators" most. But soon they're targeting each other non-stop.

Can two immature young men learn to control their "superpower" to live a normal life...and develop genuine love? Even as their relationship is threatened by the attentions of another man?

They seem just on the verge of success when a massive earthquake leaves them trapped under the rubble of their apartment in Castellammare.

With night falling and temperatures dropping, can they dig themselves out in time to save themselves? And will their injuries destroy the ability that brought them together in the first place?

Orgy at the STD Clinic

Todd Tillotson is struggling to move on after his husband is killed in a hit and run attack a year earlier during a Black Lives Matter protest in Seattle.

In this novel set entirely on public transportation, we watch as Todd, isolated throughout the pandemic, battles desperation in his attempt to safely reconnect with the world.

Will he find love again, even casual friendship, or will he simply end up another crazy old man on the bus?

Things don't look good until a man whose face he can't even see sits down beside him despite the raging variants.

And asks him a question that will change his life.

Please Evacuate

A gay, partygoing New Yorker unconcerned about the future or the unsustainability of capitalism is hit by a truck and thrust into a straight man's body half a continent away. As Hunter tries to figure out what's happening, he's caught up in another disaster, a wildfire sweeping through a Colorado community, the flames overtaking him and several schoolchildren as they flee.

When he awakens, Hunter finds himself in the body of yet another man, this time in northern Italy, a former missionary about to marry a young Mormon woman. Still piecing together this new reality, and beginning to embrace his latest identity, Hunter fights for his life in a devastating flash flood along with his wife *and* his new husband.

He's an aging worker in drought-stricken Texas, a nurse at an assisted living facility in the direct path of a hurricane, an advocate for the unhoused during a freak Seattle blizzard.

We watch as Hunter is plunged into life after life, finally recognizing the futility of only looking out for #1 and understanding the part he must play in addressing the global climate crisis...if he ever gets another chance.

Recommended Daily Humanity

A checklist of human rights must include basic housing, universal healthcare, equitable funding for public schools, and tuition-free college and vocational training.

In addition to the basics, though, we need much more to fully thrive. Subsidized childcare, universal pre-K, a universal basic income, subsidized high-speed internet, net neutrality, fare-free public transit (plus *more* public transit), and medically assisted death for the terminally ill who want it.

None of this will matter, though, if we neglect to address the rapidly worsening climate crisis.

Sound expensive? It is.

But not as expensive as refusing to implement these changes. The cost of climate disasters each year has grown to staggering figures. And the cost of social and political upheaval from not meeting the needs of suffering workers, families, and individuals may surpass even that.

It's best we understand that the vast sums required to enact meaningful change are an investment which will pay off not only in some indeterminate future but in fact almost immediately. And without these adjustments to our lifestyles and values, there may very well not be a future capable of sustaining freedom and democracy...or even civilization itself.

The Camper Killings

When a homeless man is found murdered a few blocks from Morgan Beylerian's house in south Seattle, everyone seems to consider the body just so much additional trash to be cleared from the neighborhood. But Morgan liked the guy. They used to chat when Morgan brought Nick groceries once a week.

And the brutal way the man was killed reminds Morgan of their shared Mormon heritage, back when the faithful agreed to have their throats slit if they ever revealed temple secrets.

Did Nick's former wife take action when her ex-husband refused to grant a temple divorce? Did his murder have something to do with the public accusations that brought an end to his promising career?

Morgan does his best to investigate when no one else seems to care, but it isn't easy as a man living paycheck to paycheck himself, only able to pursue his investigation via public transit.

As he continues his search for the killer, Morgan's friends withdraw and his husband threatens to leave. When another homeless man is killed and Morgan is accused of the crime, things look even bleaker.

But his troubles aren't over yet.

Will Morgan find the killer before the killer finds him?

Mormon Misfits

LGBTQ Mormons may not be a good fit for the LDS world, but there's plenty of room for them elsewhere.

A budding feminist tries to make a political statement by giving birth to her "illegitimate" son in church just before Mother's Day. A gay man works with unhoused people in Seattle while taking care of a terminally ill partner at home. A lesbian couple fight internalized homophobia that has them questioning if their desperate financial situation is a punishment from God. A man trains himself to stop praying. A gay man falls in love in Morocco. Another man learns his boyfriend was at a nightclub when a mass shooter attacked.

Few of us are a perfect fit for the culture we're born into, yet even as religious intolerance makes a desperate comeback attempt, there are good, like-minded folks everywhere. And love always wins in the end.

Gay Gaslighting

Family members and religious leaders often invoke "love" as their justification for making the lives of LGBTQ folks difficult. But we've learned how to nurture one another.

In these tales from the author of *Mormon Underwear* and *Gayrabian Nights*, a gay man invites two young Mormon missionaries to watch movies on their day off, offering R-rated and eventually X-rated films for their edification. A man receives a substantial inheritance…on the condition he leave his husband. A customer service rep at a Suicide Center established under a new theocracy "assists" those condemned of homosexuality kill themselves.

A bishop is murdered by one of his congregants for being too "liberal." A lonely wife discovers that her husband of twenty-six years is gay. Two missionaries try to interest men at an adult video store in the LDS Church. Parents tell their son he's ugly from the time they first suspect he's gay, hoping he'll be afraid to date once he becomes an adult.

As the fight to remain free of theocracy intensifies, it's important to understand what we're up against and prepare for the political—and emotional—battles ahead. One way is by telling stories oppressors don't want us to hear.

Sexual Solidarity

"Gay Ex-Mormons Unite!" In these tales by a former Mormon missionary, a polygamist in 1855 Utah is ordered to take a fourth wife, when all he really wants is to be with another man. A Victorian enthusiast has a startling sexual revelation to make at his monthly Society meeting. A gay Mormon hires a hit man in a desperate bid to stop himself from breaking the Law of Chastity.

A Relief Society president is trapped on a plane next to a gay man flaunting his sexuality. The Three Nephites seek counseling to deal with their sexual frustrations since their wives aren't immortal as they are. A worthy gay man becomes a ministering angel in the afterlife. A Mormon missionary in Italy moves in with a man he's been teaching.

Gay men don't always have lots in common, but most of us understand religious bigotry and will enjoy reading some of the many ways we've learned not only to cope but also find *"Sexual Solidarity"* with one another.

Sins of the Saints

In this collection of stories by ex-Mormon author Johnny Townsend, we see a missionary cope with the startling discovery that his companion has been translated off the face of the Earth. A teenage girl pretends to be her brother so she can "hold the priesthood" for at least a day.

A young man taught that loved ones watch over family members from the Other Side keeps imagining his grandmother catching him masturbating. A former prostitute, now a faithful Latter-day Saint, finds that some of her fellow congregants can't get beyond her past. A schizophrenic Single Adult leads a secret life no one in her congregation suspects.

Escape from Zion

In these short stories by ex-Mormon author Johnny Townsend, parents hire men to pose as the Three Nephites to teach their children the Book of Mormon is true. A shy single woman meets the man of her dreams at an endoscopy party.

An anti-Mormon mob threatens a church outing. A deceased sinner plots to break out of Spirit Prison. Aliens visiting the UN reveal that God really does live on the planet Kolob. Mormons survive the zombie apocalypse because of their two-year supply of food. A young couple desperately try to escape after America becomes a theocracy.

Another fun collection from the author of *Recommended Daily Humanity* and *Please Evacuate*.

The Mysterious Madness of Mormons

When religious indoctrination clashes with reality, the outcome can't always be predicted. In these stories by the author of *Please Evacuate* and *Inferno in the French Quarter*, a Seminary teacher threatens to kill his students. A schizophrenic woman in a hurricane evacuation shelter finds love. A Relief Society president's silicone breast implants develop into a new life form. A sister missionary suffocating under family pressure volunteers to be held hostage during a bank robbery. A teenage girl is haunted by the ghost of Emma Smith. A devout Mormon takes up sex work to raise money to help the poor.

Sometimes, behavior that seems perfectly reasonable in one culture can seem disturbing to those outside it. But whether reasonable or disturbing, their stories can also make compelling reading.

Breaking the Promise of the Promised Land: How Religious Conservatives Failed America

Many Christians in America see this country as the Promised Land, reserved for them and them only. They want a theocracy. Almost every decision is made to exert more control over citizens of every faith. Their punitive, coercive policies have caused mass suffering which they blame on the people they've crushed.

Religious conservatives have failed America.

Political conservatism has been transformed into religious dogma and dogma into public policy. And any politician—or friend or family member—who expresses the tiniest dissent from increasingly harsh theocratic ideals is instantly demonized and shunned into compliance.

What the rest of us must do is focus on human-centered solutions. We need universal healthcare, tuition-free college and vocational training, subsidized childcare, fare-free public transit, a living wage, universal basic income, and an immediate ban on all new fossil fuel projects.

Because the far right and corporate collaborators on the left have already brought so much destruction, our options are now limited to taxing corporations and the wealthy to pay their fair share or accepting we'll live in an increasingly dystopian society.

Equity and justice aren't free, and in these essays, author Johnny Townsend (*Recommended Daily Humanity, Am I My Planet's Keeper?*) shows us that no matter the cost, they're still cheaper than the alternative.

Kinky Quilts

Since patchwork quilts are usually displayed in bedrooms where couples engage in sex, why are there so few quilt designs for folks who want a bit of sexual energy in these intimate spaces?

The original designs in this volume range from simple to intermediate, and with over 250 to choose from, even beginner quilters will find patterns tempting enough to get started.

In *Kinky Quilts*, Johnny Townsend has collected his best designs from *Quilting Beyond the Rainbow, Gay Sleeping Arrangements*, and *Queer Quilting*, to offer fun, sexy quilts for men who love men.

Please Evacuate Again

As Craig and Toby struggle to keep their faltering marriage alive, the climate crisis intrudes, part of a threesome in their relationship.

Craig wants to take drastic action but Toby just wants to live his life as best he can before climate breakdown escalates.

"You fight for your life by any means necessary," Craig insists. "If someone breaks into your house, you pull out a baseball bat or a gun. When there's a mass shooting, you run, hide, or fight back."

But when it involves global warming? And fossil fuel industries buying politicians who protect carbon emissions at the cost of human lives?

Craig wonders if a letter to the editor is effective. If blocking traffic at a rally once or twice a year is enough.

Toby threatens to leave him if does anything stupid. And to report him to the authorities.

But Craig feels he'll need to commit violence one way or another, either by condoning the status quo or by doing whatever he can to fight those who keep destabilizing the climate. So he joins a group of eco activists whose efforts are far more extreme than even he had expected.

Will Craig survive the violent police crackdown on protesters?

Will his relationship with Toby survive the additional stress of betrayal?

And will either of them survive the new wildfire that's just started at the edge of town?

What Readers Have Said

Townsend's stories are "a gay *Portnoy's Complaint* of Mormonism. Salacious, sweet, sad, insightful, insulting, religiously ethnic, quirky-faithful, and funny."

D. Michael Quinn, author of *The Mormon Hierarchy: Origins of Power*

"Told from a believably conversational first-person perspective, [*A Gay Mormon Missionary in Pompeii*'s] novelistic focus on Anderson's journey to thoughtful self-acceptance allows for greater character development than often seen in short stories, which makes this well-paced work rich and satisfying, and one of Townsend's strongest. An extremely important contribution to the field of Mormon fiction." Named to Kirkus Reviews' Best of 2011.

Kirkus Reviews

"The thirteen stories in *Mormon Underwear* capture this struggle [between Mormonism and homosexuality] with humor, sadness, insight, and sometimes shocking details....*Mormon Underwear* provides compelling stories, literally from the inside-out."

Niki D'Andrea, *Phoenix New Times*

"Townsend's lively writing style and engaging characters [in *Zombies for Jesus*] make for stories which force us to wake up, smell the (prohibited) coffee, and review our attitudes with regard to reading dogma so doggedly. These are tales which revel in the individual tics and quirks which make us human, Mormon or not, gay or not..."

A.J. Kirby, *The Short Review*

"The Rift," from *A Gay Mormon Missionary in Pompeii*, is a "fascinating tale of an untenable situation...a *tour de force.*"

David Lenson, editor, *The Massachusetts Review*

"Pronouncing the Apostrophe," from *The Golem of Rabbi Loew*, is "quiet and revealing, an intriguing tale..."

Sima Rabinowitz, Literary Magazine Review, *NewPages.com*

The Circumcision of God is "a collection of short stories that consider the imperfect, silenced majority of Mormons, who may in fact be [the Church's] best hope....[The book leaves] readers regretting the church's willingness to marginalize those who best exemplify its ideals: those who love fiercely despite all obstacles, who brave challenges at great personal risk and who always choose the hard, higher road."

Kirkus Reviews

In *Mormon Fairy Tales*, Johnny Townsend displays "both a wicked sense of irony and a deep well of compassion."

Kel Munger, *Sacramento News and Review*

Zombies for Jesus is "eerie, erotic, and magical."

Publishers Weekly

"While [Townsend's] many touching vignettes draw deeply from Mormon mythology, history, spirituality and culture, [*Mormon Fairy Tales*] is neither a gaudy act of proselytism nor angry protest literature from an ex-believer. Like all good fiction, his stories are simply about the joys, the hopes and the sorrows of people."

Kirkus Reviews

"In *Inferno in the French Quarter* author Johnny Townsend restores this tragic event [the UpStairs Lounge fire] to its proper place in LGBT history and reminds us that the victims of the blaze were not just 'statistics,' but real people with real lives, families, and friends."

Jesse Monteagudo, *The Bilerico Project*

In *Inferno in the French Quarter*, "Townsend's heart-rending descriptions of the victims...seem to [make them] come alive once more."

Kit Van Cleave, *OutSmart Magazine*

"While [*Inferno in the French Quarter*] is a non-fiction work, the author is a skilled fiction [writer], so he manages to respect the realism of the story, while at the same time recreating their lives and voices. It's probably thanks to the [author's] skills that this piece of non-fiction goes well beyond a simple recording of events."

Elisa Rolle, *Rainbow Awards*

Marginal Mormons is "an irreverent, honest look at life outside the mainstream Mormon Church....Throughout his musings on sin and forgiveness, Townsend beautifully demonstrates his characters' internal, perhaps irreconcilable struggles....Rather than anger and disdain, he offers an honest portrayal of people searching for meaning and community in their lives, regardless of their life choices or secrets." Named to Kirkus Reviews' Best of 2012.

Kirkus Reviews

The stories in *The Mormon Victorian Society* "register the new openness and confidence of gay life in the age of same-sex marriage....What hasn't changed is Townsend's wry, conversational prose, his subtle evocations of character and social dynamics, and his deadpan humor. His warm empathy still glows in this intimate yet clear-eyed engagement with Mormon theology and folkways. Funny, shrewd and finely wrought dissections of the awkward contradictions—and surprising harmonies—between conscience and desire." Named to Kirkus Reviews' Best of 2013.

Kirkus Reviews

"This collection of short stories [*The Mormon Victorian Society*] featuring gay Mormon characters slammed [me] in the face from the first page, wrestled my heart and mind to the floor, and left me panting and wanting more by the end. Johnny Townsend has created so many memorable characters in such few pages. I went weeks thinking about this book. It truly touched me."

Tom Webb, *A Bear on Books*

Dragons of the Book of Mormon is an "entertaining collection....Townsend's prose is sharp, clear, and easy to read, and his characters are well rendered..."

Publishers Weekly

"The pre-eminent documenter of alternative Mormon lifestyles...Townsend has a deep understanding of his characters, and his limpid prose, dry humor and well-grounded (occasionally magical) realism make their spiritual conundrums both compelling and entertaining. [*Dragons of the Book of Mormon* is] [a]nother of Townsend's critical but affectionate and absorbing tours of Mormon discontent." Named to Kirkus Reviews' Best of 2014.

Kirkus Reviews

In *Gayrabian Nights*, "Townsend's prose is always limpid and evocative, and…he finds real drama and emotional depth in the most ordinary of lives."

Kirkus Reviews

Gayrabian Nights is a "complex revelation of how seriously soul damaging the denial of the true self can be."

Ryan Rhodes, author of *Free Electricity*

Gayrabian Nights "was easily the most original book I've read all year. Funny, touching, topical, and thoroughly enjoyable."

Rainbow Awards

Lying for the Lord is "one of the most gripping books that I've picked up for quite a while. I love the author's writing style, alternately cynical, humorous, biting, scathing, poignant, and touching…. This is the third book of his that I've read, and all are equally engaging. These are stories that need to be told, and the author does it in just the right way."

Heidi Alsop, *Ex-Mormon Foundation Board Member*

In *Lying for the Lord*, Townsend "gets under the skin of his characters to reveal their complexity and conflicts....shrewd, evocative [and] wryly humorous."

Kirkus Reviews

In *Missionaries Make the Best Companions*, "the author treats the clash between religious dogma and liberal humanism with vivid realism, sly humor, and subtle feeling as his characters try to figure out their true missions in life. Another of Townsend's rich dissections of Mormon failures and uncertainties..." Named to Kirkus Reviews' Best of 2015.

Kirkus Reviews

In *Invasion of the Spirit Snatchers*, "Townsend, a confident and practiced storyteller, skewers the hypocrisies and eccentricities of his characters with precision and affection. The outlandish framing narrative is the most consistent source of shock and humor, but the stories do much to ground the reader in the world—or former world—of the characters....A funny, charming tale about a group of Mormons facing the end of the world."

Kirkus Reviews

"Townsend's collection [*The Washing of Brains*] once again displays his limpid, naturalistic prose, skillful narrative chops, and his subtle insights into psychology...Well-crafted dispatches on the clash between religion and self-fulfillment..."

Kirkus Reviews

"While the author is generally at his best when working as a satirist, there are some fine, understated touches in these tales [*The Last Days Linger*] that will likely affect readers in subtle ways....readers should come away impressed by the deep empathy he shows for all his characters—even the homophobic ones."

Kirkus Reviews

"Written in a conversational style that often uses stories and personal anecdotes to reveal larger truths, this immensely approachable book [*Racism by Proxy*] skillfully serves its intended audience of White readers grappling with complex questions regarding race, history, and identity. The author's frequent references to the Church of Jesus Christ of Latter-day Saints may be too niche for readers unfamiliar with its idiosyncrasies, but Townsend generally strikes a perfect balance of humor, introspection, and reasoned arguments that will engage even skeptical readers."

Kirkus Reviews

Orgy at the STD Clinic portrays "an all-too real scenario that Townsend skewers to wincingly accurate proportions…[with] instant classic moments courtesy of his punchy, sassy, sexy lead character…"

Jim Piechota, *Bay Area Reporter*

Orgy at the STD Clinic is "…a triumph of humane sensibility. A richly textured saga that brilliantly captures the fraying social fabric of contemporary life." Named to Kirkus Reviews' Best Indie Books of 2022.

Kirkus Reviews

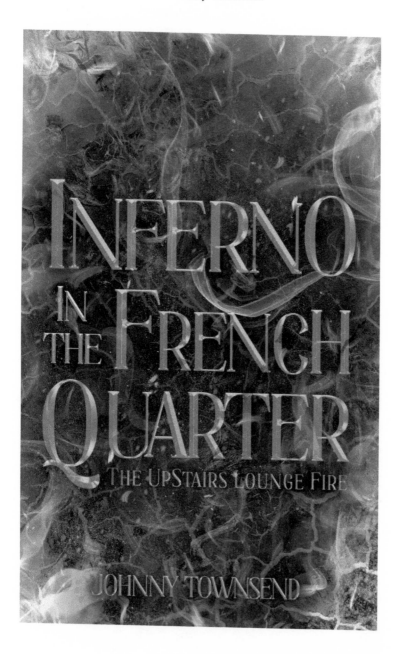